CHICAGO BULLS

STAMPEDE!

A REMARKABLE RUN
TO THE 1991 NBA TITLE

First printing, July 1991

For information about this and other Sentinel
and Tribune Media Services books, contact:

Sentinel Books
P.O. 1100
Orlando, Florida 32802-1100

Library of Congress Catalog Card Number:
91-062489
ISBN 0-941263-33-9

We started from
the bottom, and it was hard working our
way to the top. But we did it.'

Michael Jordan
of the 1991 NBA champion
Chicago Bulls

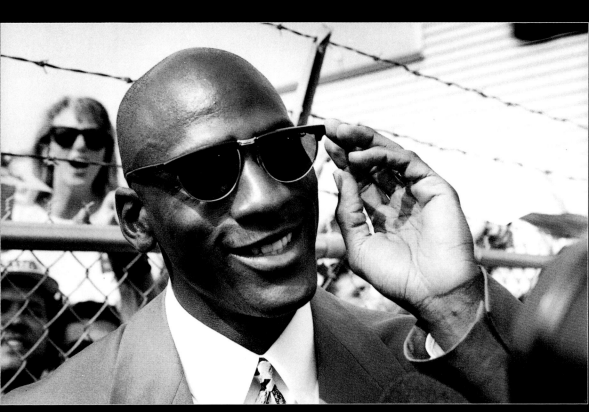

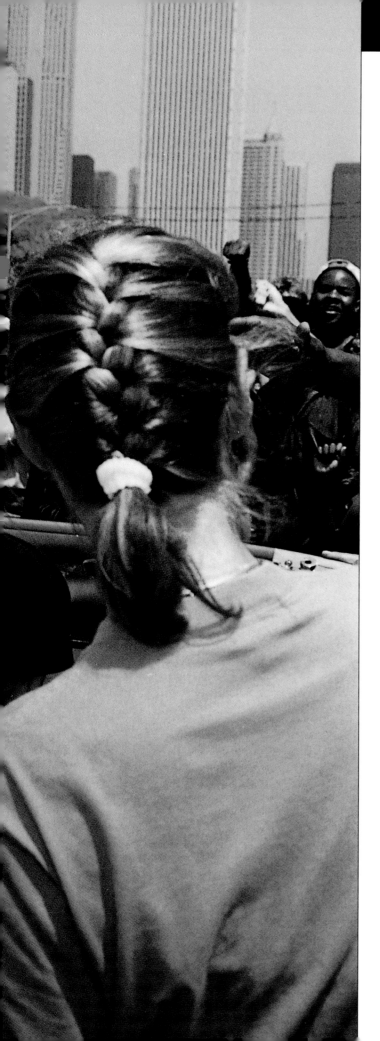

By the time they finished a compelling post-game prayer on championship night, the Chicago Bulls caught the eyes —and emotions —of those fans who watched the team play in 1990-91.

From grandmothers to school kids to the second-balcony faithful, the Bulls provided something for everyone during their stampede through the regular season and playoffs.

You want excitement? Flip to Michael Jordan's incredible move in Game 2 of the NBA Finals.

Looking for drama? Travel to Los Angeles for the Friday night overtime of Game 3 with the Lakers. Clutch shooting? Check out John Paxson's field goal percentage for the championship series.

How about poise under pressure? See the file on coach Phil Jackson and his young but mature pair of forwards, Scottie Pippen and Horace Grant. And don't forget to look up veteran center Bill Cartwright, who endured plenty of skeptics to earn his championship ring after 12 seasons in the league.

Care for some noise? Listen to the spotlight introductions at Chicago Stadium. A little peace and quiet? Consider a nation respectfully watching Craig Hodges lead his teammates in The Lord's Prayer as network cameras rolled after Game 5.

Maybe you like a good cry. Fast-forward to Jordan's trophy tears of joy in the winning locker room.

Or perhaps you simply appreciate the rewards of patience and hard work and solid game plans. Then sit down with this book and savor the memories of the first NBA title in the Chicago Bulls' 25-year history, month by month, piece by championship piece.

It has a little something for everyone.

–BOB CONDOR
CHICAGO, JUNE 1991

John Paxson and his wife, Carolyn, are mobbed by adoring fans en route to the team's rally at Grant Park.
PHOTO BY MICHAEL MEINHARDT

TEAMWORK

he 1990-91 Bulls' NBA championship was a journey, of sorts, that started one June morning back in 1984.

For that was when the Bulls selected Michael Jordan in the annual NBA draft of the top collegiate players. Jordan was merely among the best then, selected third by the Bulls, who never realized just how good he could become or how far he could help take them.

But it would be an arduous road, chock full of bumpy coaching changes and drastic personnel shifts. It would be a long, slow trip. But even Jordan believed reaching the destination would then be that much more rewarding.

"I know I'm going to appreciate it more if, and when, it comes," Jordan had said earlier in the 1990-91 season, "because I was there at the beginning, when we were on the bottom."

The Bulls reached the top in June by dominating the Los Angeles Lakers in the NBA Finals.

Phil Jackson, with his wonderfully relaxed style and hyperkinetic defensive notions, had brought with him an offensive system that featured Jordan while allowing the guys in the band to have their solos.

The Bulls—led by Jordan and fellow starters Scottie Pippen, Horace Grant, Bill Cartwright and John Paxson—became a team under their coach in the playoffs, although along the way their feats were not to be overlooked: A franchise-best 61 wins and a Central Division crown and an all-time record home winning streak.

The Bulls were on the cusp of greatness all season. They made others take notice in the playoffs when they came within two desperate three-point field goals of sweeping to a title. They whipped the Knicks and lost just one of five games with Philadelphia. They shut out the hated Pistons and nearly did the same to the proud Lakers.

They were too quick, too accurate with their shots and too aggressive in their play. They won with finesse and flash, with a little bit of dash and a little dirt. The Bulls did everything required of champions and now wear the crown proudly. –SAM SMITH

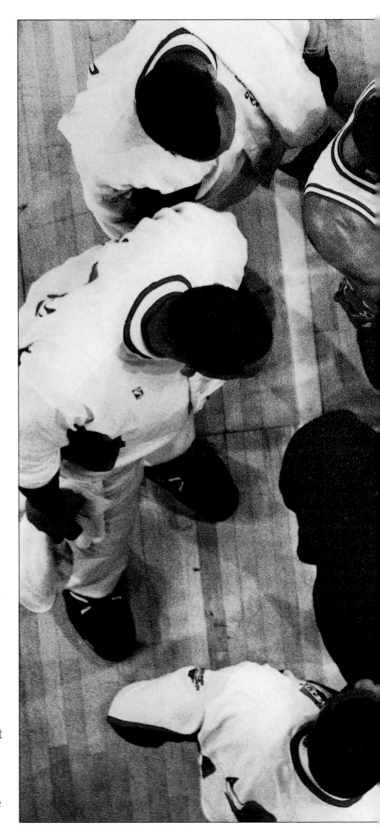

Phil Jackson, a coach with a deft touch all season, leads the team during a timeout.
PHOTO BY CHARLES CHERNEY

JORDA

He wasn't the big man everyone wanted, but Michael Jordan becoming a Bull in June 1984 was a giant leap for the franchise. Just six weeks into Jordan's rookie year, Chicago fans saw a superstar blast off. Six seasons later, Jordan and the Bulls were poised to soar even higher.

IN

Hi mom!

Michael For President

PHOTOS BY CHARLES CHERNEY AND JIM PRISCHING (LEFT)

PHOTOS BY CARL WAGNER (TOP), PAUL F. GERO (RIGHT) AND CHARLES OSGOOD (BELOW)

Chicago has been Michael Jordan's kind of town since he arrived as a rookie in 1984. Swinging with the Sox or playing golf for charity, he's been Chicago's kind of guy too.

Air mail: Destination bulls

n the beginning was the word and the word was this: To win big in the NBA, you have to have a big man. If God had been an NBA general manager, he never would have chosen Moses to lead the Israelites to the Promised Land. He would have drafted whoever was the Goliath of that time.

Six weeks after the Bulls made Michael Jordan the third choice in the 1984 draft, the word already was being rewritten.

"In two or three years," said George Raveling, who was then assistant coach of the U.S. Olympic basketball team, "there's going to be a major controversy in the NBA. It will concern how Michael Jordan was allowed to be drafted third instead of second or first."

The two men drafted ahead of him, of course, were big men. The Houston Rockets, drafting first, chose Hakeem Olajuwon, as everyone knew they would. The powerful 7-foot center had led the University of Houston to the NCAA final two years in a row.

Next up was Portland, which had been indicating in the weeks before the draft it was going to take Sam Bowie, a 7-1 center who had come back from a broken leg to help take Kentucky to the Final Four.

Bowie was a bit of a risk. There was the leg problem. There also was the fact Bowie, along with the rest of his team, had played miserably in the NCAA semifinals against Georgetown and Patrick Ewing.

"Portland gets a lot of criticism for that pick," says Bulls General Manager Jerry Krause. "I think it's false

Michael Jordan, whose play has always been big, slams home another basket.
PHOTO BY MILBERT ORLANDO BROWN

By Robert Markus

criticism. If I had Clyde Drexler and if you believe Bowie is a player, and he's 7-1, you have to take the big guy. If I didn't have Drexler, sure, I'd have taken Michael."

So Jordan fell into the Bulls' lap. Manna from heaven. Right up until draft day, then-General Manager Rod Thorn had explored trade possibilities. One deal would have sent the pick to Dallas for hometown hero Terry Cummings, a 6-9 power forward who had played at De Paul.

Another would have brought center Tree Rollins from Atlanta, solving what was thought to be the most critical problem. After all, if you want to win big in the NBA, you need a big man—don't you?

Thorn, who says he would have chosen Olajuwon, but not Bowie, over Jordan, decided to keep the draft pick. With a crowd of Bulls fans in the draft headquarters at the Hilton hotel chanting "Jordan, Jordan," Thorn gave the throng what it wanted.

He also gave Chicago the most electrifying performer in sports. And he gave the lie, it seems, to the word, which in the beginning was: If you want to win big, draft big. For in seven years, Jordan, the biggest 6-6 player in the history of basketball, has transformed the Bulls.

They had not made the playoffs in the three years before Jordan arrived. They have not failed to make them since. They had not played to a single sellout crowd, home or away, in two seasons before he came.

Within two years they were selling out regularly, and for the last two years there has not been a ticket available for any Bulls game, home or away.

And, of course, they never had advanced to the NBA Finals. The little miracles Jordan performed almost immediately. The major miracle took him seven years.

He didn't do it alone and he knew all along he could not. He said as much from the day he showed up to sign his contract, the largest in the history of the team.

But the truth is, he could do such wondrous things with a basketball in his hands that it sometimes looked as if he could do it all by himself.

Take that day in Boston: April 21, 1986. The day he scored 63 points against the Celtics. In the playoffs. The day Celtics coach K.C. Jones looked down his bench to find someone to guard Jordan because Dennis Johnson, who was trying to do it, was being destroyed. Jones remembers: "Every other time I'd ever looked down the bench, guys would be leaning forward hoping to catch my eye so I'd put them in. This time everybody was hiding. Nobody wanted to go into the game."

The day when, after it was over, the great Larry Bird would say: "That was the most amazing display of basketball I've ever seen. Right here in Boston, in the Garden, on national TV, God came down disguised as Michael Jordan."

OK, so the Bulls lost that day, 135-131 in double overtime. The fact is one man—and not a big man—almost singlehandedly had beaten a team that would go on to win the NBA title.

Or take the day in Cleveland three years later when the underdog Bulls were down to their last three seconds, trailing the hometown Cavaliers by a point in the fifth and deciding game of the opening round of the playoffs. Everyone in the place knew the ball was going to Jordan.

Here come three Cavaliers flying to meet him. He grabs the inbounds pass and leaves one defender grasping the air. Another gets there too late. But the third is right in his face as he takes two dribbles, soars in the air, moving from right to left, and sends the ball cleanly through the net from 17 feet away. Bulls 101, Cavs 100.

Wherever he goes, Jordan draws attention, this time from Philly's Rick Mahorn. PHOTO BY BOB LANGER

Seldom has any player in any sport created such an instant sensation as did Jordan when he arrived in Chicago. His performance in the Olympics had only whetted the appetites of victory-starved Bulls fans.

"Michael is like an artist," said Raveling after watching Jordan lead the United States to a gold medal. "Most players lack creativity, even some of the great ones. Michael brings to the game creativity and originality. When he puts the ball to the floor, no one, including Michael, knows what will happen. But it's usually spectacular."

Chicago fans got their first look at him in the preseason.

"At Gary, Ind., they about tore the gym down trying to get at him," remembers Bulls director of media services Tim Hallam. "The word spread like wildfire. It was like a plane crashing. People knew immediately."

What they knew was that no longer would they have to wait for Julius Erving's rare visits to the Stadium to see magic. Houdini was in their midst, and they could wallow in it. Forgotten would be all those years of futility when the Bulls were among the worst teams in the league.

In the preceding nine years the Bulls, after climbing almost to the top under Dick Motta, had fallen hard. They had only two winning seasons in all that time, only two trips to the playoffs. And even those two "good" years were not that good.

In 1977 they were 10 games under .500 until winning 20 of their last 24. Four years later they won 13 of their last 15 to finish eight games above .500. That was all that had broken nine years of depressing defeat.

Now Jordan was here and the sun would come up tomorrow. The fans were sure of it. And they were right.

In his third regular-season game as a Bull, Jordan scored 37 points. For the first time, the Bulls sent Hallam on the road to help Jordan handle the crush of the media.

"Every city we went," Hallam recalls, "they'd have a room already arranged and he'd do a half-hour press conference, then do one-on-ones for radio and TV."

> **'Right here in Boston, on national TV, God came down disguised as Michael Jordan.'**
> **- Larry Bird**

Within six weeks his picture was on the cover of Sports Illustrated. "Sid Green and Orlando Woolridge used to say it was like traveling with Michael Jackson," Hallam says.

Now Jordan may be bigger than Michael Jackson. Between his basketball salary and his endorsements, Jordan has pocketed an estimated $65 million in his pro career. Jordan's sensational moves, his remarkable hang time, his drives to the basket with his tongue hanging out, his gravity-defying dunks, his clean-cut good looks and pleasant manner made him an instant superstar.

But underneath was a competitive fire that at times was almost too hot to handle. His college roommate, Buzz Peterson, recalls that Jordan once became so enraged after losing at Monopoly that he threw his remaining play money in Peterson's face and stalked out of the room.

"Because of Michael's competitiveness," says Krause, "we've had to build with different types of individuals. We've brought in some players who weren't tough enough to compete with him in practice. We had to get rid of them.

"I never thought I'd see anyone play as hard in

'I never thought I'd see anyone play as hard in practice as Jerry Sloan. But Michael does.'
- Jerry Krause

Michael Jordan and Horace Grant prepare to enter a 1989 game.
PHOTO BY CHARLES CHERNEY

practice as Jerry Sloan. But Michael does. He's uncompromising."

In one practice in his rookie year, Jordan got so angry at coach Kevin Loughery he nearly walked out. Loughery had a habit of ending each practice with a five-on-five scrimmage to 11 baskets, the losing team sentenced to run 15 laps. On this occasion, Jordan's red team was ahead 7-2 when Loughery ordered Jordan to turn his shirt inside out and finish with the white team.

Fuming, Jordan considered leaving. Instead he scored seven baskets in a row and the white team won 11-8. "I was trying to challenge him and test him," Loughery said.

Years later, Jordan would reflect, "Loughery may have been the best coach I've had here, for me. He pushed me to limits I didn't think I could reach."

Jordan, in turn, has pushed the Bulls to limits few ever thought they could reach. As great as he is, "No team has ever won an NBA championship built around a guard," says Krause. "It has never been done. It's easier to build around power players."

Yet there was never any question Jordan was the player around whom the rest of the team would have to revolve. It was Jordan who put points on the board and people in the seats.

Try as he might, Krause can find no one moment when it became apparent Jordan could lead the team to the title.

"If there is one point, one of the things that has happened is that Michael's own mentality has changed," says Krause. "I think he has a greater appreciation now of what the other guys do.

"For Michael to do the things he does, guys have to set screens. Guys have to dive for the ball. When the game's on the line, guys have to say, 'It's Michael's ball.' There has to be some sacrifice on the team's part. But also on Michael's part. He had to learn that those guys were busting their butts to get it done for him."

Jordan, as Krause puts it, "has gotten out of the air-show business." The crowd-pleasing dunks still come, but more and more they come off defensive pressure he has helped create.

So Jordan has performed yet another miracle. He has gotten out of the air-show business yet elevated his game to an even higher level. And he has carried the Bulls with him—up, up, higher than they ever have been. – **BOB SAKAMOTO CONTRIBUTED TO THIS STORY**

HOW DOES MICHAEL FLY?

▶ Or does he really? Is hang time an illusion? ▶ How high could Michael fly untethered on the moon? ▶ Michael and the parabola: The mechanics of Air Jordan's flight.

▶ Look! Up in the sky

The ability to soar to unique heights has put Michael Jordan, the master of hang time, in a class by himself. Skill plus speed and physics allow Michael to do the seemingly impossible. Tremendous thigh and calf muscle strength are only part of what makes Michael fly. His jumping creativity and ever-changing aerobatics leave even the best defenders frustrated. Each jump is marked with the special Jordan style, but one thing that Michael can't beat is the law of gravity, which he nevertheless tries to defy every time he leaps.

▶ Cleared for landing, Mr. Jordan

$-\frac{1}{2} g_z T^2 + v_0 T = \text{ALTITUDE}$

There's more than one way to look at the magic Michael does. Lt. Col. Douglas Kirkpatrick, a professor of astronautics with the Air Force, has used algebraic equations to study Jordan's jumps and acknowledges that Michael's abilities are phenomenal, but he has a more down-to-earth explanation. "There's nothing specific about his flight that makes his hang time any different than anyone else's. If you look at what he does in slow motion, you'll see he does glide and make it look like he's floating. But there's nothing anyone can do to hang longer. Hang time is a misnomer."

▶ Just hanging around

No conversation about Michael Jordan is complete without references to hang time. So, what exactly is hang time? The velocity, or speed, a player has when he takes off, combined with the path his center of gravity follows on the way up, plus body manipulations along the way, fool us into thinking he's hanging in the air for an unusually long period of time. Calculated with Jordan's vertical jump of 48 inches, the total amount of time he's in the air during a jump is approximately one second. Fast speed coming into the jump simply gives the jumper added momentum. Jordan's vertical speed is much greater than that of the average athlete, and what he does in the air—motioning his arms from below his waist to above his head and spreading his legs—creates the illusion.

▶ The physics of a jump

THE PARABOLA

Vertical speed is zero

A simple geometric parabola illustrates the path, or trajectory, a jumper's center of gravity (roughly at his waist) takes during a jump. The jumper can be considered a projectile, the object that is launched upward. The size and shape of the trajectory depends entirely on the launching speed and angle—the lower the angle of the trajectory the sooner the object will hit the ground. Based on Isaac Newton's laws, we know that what comes up must come down and that gravity affects only vertical, not horizontal movement. At the peak of the jump, vertical speed is close to or at zero, which explains the illusion of a jumper hanging in the air as if it motionless.

▶ Gravity fighters

There's no such thing as defying gravity. Based on Isaac Newton's study of gravity in the 1600s, the force of gravity on any object is equal to the weight of that object. Once a projectile leaves the ground, the path its center of gravity follows is set. The combination of Jordan's body position when he leaves the ground, his position when he recontacts the ground and movements along the way create the illusion.

▶ Michael in orbit

Based on Jordan's 11,000-plus points and about 5,500 jumps, Lt. Col. Kirkpatrick figured Michael has been airborne for 1½ hours during his five years with the Bulls. That's the length of an airplane flight from Chicago to Buffalo, and one low-altitude orbit around the earth for the space shuttle. Kirkpatrick's formula was reworked from original calculations, which had Michael in the air six hours, enough for four low-altitude earth orbits.

The view from above

"I don't know for certain about hang time. I think it's more or less a motion that makes it look like you're hanging. That's something I tend to have more than other people. The motion of my legs and my arms, my aerobatics, looks as though I'm hanging in the air longer than normal. But I don't think I actually that I am."

—MICHAEL ON MICHAEL

The Jordan style

When it comes to technique, Jordan's flight patterns can't be duplicated. "I just make it up," he admits. For every crowd-pleasing cradle jam or rock-a-baby dunk Jordan does, there are countless others that have yet to be named. Winner of back-to-back NBA Slam Dunk Championships in 1987 and 1988, Jordan has risen to the top of his class.

Jordan dunk-ology

A brief list of classic Jordan dunks:
- Cradle jam
- Rock-a-baby
- Demoralizer
- Leaner (below)
- Tomahawk (right)

▶ The muscle behind the magic

High center of gravity — Slender torso
Muscular thighs — Quadriceps

Jordan plays a lot of basketball. But off the court, he does little to strengthen his body. For example, he does no weight-training. So how is it he's able to hit the heights he does? Michael's rocket-powered leaps are helped by long legs and a slender torso, which give him a higher center of gravity. However, it's the makeup of his muscles, mainly the quadriceps, calf muscles and gluteus, that gives him the power.

A good jumper will have muscles that store elastic energy and also a larger percentage of fast-twitch than slow-twitch fibers. Fast-twitch fibers provide a quick burst of explosive power, while slow-twitch fibers are more useful for endurance. The best jumpers tend to have a higher ratio of fast-twitch to slow-twitch fibers, while the opposite is true of marathon runners. Like a spring, jumping muscles store and release elastic energy. During a jump the quadriceps contracts, which straightens the knee and hip joints. Stored elastic energy adds to the process and leads to the energy of motion.

Stages of a vertical jump

18 in.
48 in.

▶ Have body will fly

At 6-6, Jordan's center of gravity is higher than that of the average person and his aerial acrobatics cause it to rise even higher during a jump. The terrific force he exerts on the floor gives him a quick takeoff and longer time in the air. Biomechanical researchers have concluded that a good jumper produces an average force of about two to three times his weight pushing off the ground.

▶ Jumping to the max

On any given leap, Jordan, who weighs about 200 pounds, is exerting 400 to 600 pounds of force on the floor. Compare that to Atlanta's Spud Webb, who at 5-7 and 135 jumps 42 inches vertically and exerts 270 to 400 pounds of force.

Moon-jumping

Since objects on the moon weigh one-sixth what they do on earth, a jumper can rise six times higher and remain in flight six times longer than on earth. So, weighing in at a nearly 33 pounds, Jordan would perform vertical leaps of 24 feet!

Michael on the moon — 24 ft.

Michael on earth — 48 in.
Spud on earth — 42 in.

Chicago Tribune Graphic by Dennis Odom and Julie Sheer; Sources: Michael Jordan; Lt. Col. Douglas Kirkpatrick; Peter Van Handel; Steve Ingram; Jesus Dapena; Gordon Valiant; Sport Science, by Peter J. Brancazio; Photo reference/Ed Wagner, Jr.

NOVE

The season started with three straight losses. Not exactly championship material. The first win was a struggle against the Timberwolves, of all teams. By month's end, the Bulls, especially the newly equipped Horace Grant, saw their way clear to starting a seven-game win streak.

PHOTO BY ED WAGNER

MBER

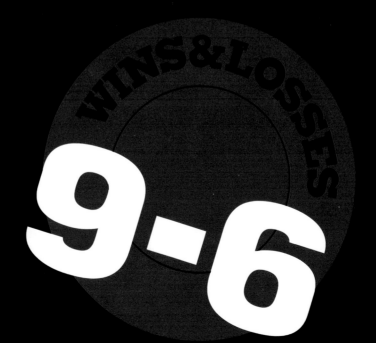

WINS&LOSSES

9-6

**Michael Jordan couldn't run away from a 124-116 season-opening loss to Philadelphia.
PHOTO BY CHARLES CHERNEY**

T he season began with a lesson in humility, taught by the Philadelphia 76ers. The Sixers, 124-116 winners at the Stadium, made the Bulls "look like chumps," Michael Jordan said. Perhaps Philly deserved the Bulls' thanks, for they showed them the path to the NBA championship — hard work.

HEY, YOU BUNCH OF FATHEADS!

Bernie Lincicome

IN THE WAKE OF THE NEWS

What the Bulls need right about now is a good insult.

"Please do," said Michael Jordan. "I can't wait to start hearing the boos."

I'll do what I can.

HEY, YOU BUNCH OF LAZY FATHEADS! YOU CLUMSY NOSEPICKERS! WHAT ARE YOU DOING, COUNTING YOUR MONEY OR ADMIRING YOUR PRESS CLIPPINGS? YOU SURE AIN'T PLAYING BASKETBALL.

"I love that stuff," said Jordan. "I really do."

THIS IS THE NEW AND IMPROVED BULLS? ARE THOSE HANDS OR HOOVES? TRYING THE NEW, FLO-THRU LIPTON DEFENSE, ARE YOU?

This is necessary because the Bulls, the heir apparent Bulls, the infant dynasty Bulls, have not learned how to take a compliment.

"Maybe the worst thing that happened," said Phil Jackson, the coach, "is we spent the week before the first game in Chicago listening to everybody tell us how we are going to win the NBA championship."

Reality is named Charles Barkley, he of the Philadelphia 76ers. Barkley sent the Bulls off into their season of destiny opening night with a smirk, a grunt and more points than the original Jordan himself.

"Philadelphia made us look like chumps," Jordan said.

CHUMPS? YOU GUYS LOOKED LIKE THE BOTTOM OF A BAT CAVE! AND SMELLED WORSE!

There are more Barkleys waiting, assorted Birds and Ewings and Laimbeers, unimpressed with preseason logic and an automatic trip for the Bulls to the Finals.

"You'd think the Finals were starting tomorrow without having a season," grumbled Jordan.

HEY, HORACE GRANT, THOSE NEW GOGGLES HELP YOU SEE HOW FAR YOU MISS YOUR FREE THROWS?

This little matter of having to play a season was easy to overlook, a nuisance for near-champions like the Bulls, a team definitely on the rise.

Didn't the Bulls fix what they needed to fix, got some experience on the bench, just like Jordan demanded after that goofy, gloomy Game 7 surrender in Auburn Hills?

CLIFF LEVINGSTON, TRY SEEING WHAT THE FRONT OF BARKLEY'S JERSEY LOOKS LIKE!

B.J. ARMSTRONG, CROSS YOUR LEGS SITTING ON THE BENCH, NOT WHEN YOU ARE DRIBBLING!

STACEY KING, IF YOU TRY SHOOTING FROM ABOVE THE BASKET, IT WON'T GET BLOCKED BY SOMEBODY'S KNEE!

New players, better players, improved strategy. The Bulls are full of 'em. Here's a new idea: Let somebody besides Jordan do all the scoring. Spread the playing time around. Put Jordan on the bench for 14 minutes. Rest him up for April in November.

"Everybody seems to be more concerned about my playing time than I am," Jordan said.

HEY, GENIUS JACKSON, THE KIDS ARE HERE TO HELP JORDAN GET HIS RING. PLAY JORDAN 34 MINUTES AGAINST MINNESOTA, AGAINST ORLANDO, AGAINST THE LOS ANGELES CLIPPERS. AGAINST SOMEBODY WHO MATTERS, LET HIM BE MICHAEL JORDAN! WHAT'D YOU DO ON YOUR VACATION, PAINT A MUSTACHE ON THE MONA LISA?

"I don't mind losing the opening game," said Jackson. "It's good for a club to see what it's made of."

Might I suggest. . . .HOT AIR!

"We have been a little full of ourselves," Jordan said.

"We're only human," Jackson said. "When you get patted on the back all the time, it's hard not to think you are better than you are."

SCOTTIE PIPPEN! TAKE AN ASPIRIN!

WILL PERDUE, YOUR PARKING METER HAS EXPIRED!

I hope I have been of some help. ∎

LOOKING GOOD

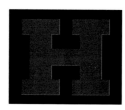 e was up to 235 pounds, almost 20 more than he weighed during the 1989-90 season. After a rigorous summer, he was bench-pressing and squat-lifting more than 300 pounds, numbers usually associated with pro football players.

"His lifting and strength are comparable to a defensive end's," said Bulls strength coach Al Vermeil, who worked for the San Francisco 49ers 10 years ago. "He's similar to the bigger, lankier players."

Horace Grant came into the Bulls' championship season stronger and tougher. He had to be because NBA players have no qualms about bumping a guy who wears glasses.

Grant donned protective goggles in 1990-91 and began wearing glasses off the court. An exam before the season found he had vision too poor to drive a car.

"When I finally did get my eyes checked, they found out I was driving illegally," he said. "My vision is terrible. I knew I needed glasses, but I tried contacts in college and they didn't agree with me, so I didn't wear

Horace Grant added 20 pounds of muscle, and new eyewear, to a newfound maturity.
PHOTO BY JIM PRISCHING

anything for a long period of time."

To the fan, no problem was apparent. Grant raised his scoring average from 7.7 as a rookie to 13.4 in 1989-90 and his rebounding mark from 5.5 to 7.9.

But the coaches saw things Grant apparently didn't. Like flying basketballs.

"We'd see a lot of things happen and we'd wonder, 'Gee, why didn't he just pick that ball out of the air and put it back in?'" coach Phil Jackson said.

Assistant coach John Bach had studied Grant on and off the court and had raised the point.

"You'd see him reading the newspaper and he'd have it smack up against his face," Bach said.

"It was coach Bach who kept pushing for me to get my eyes checked out," Grant said. "And it's a big difference. Now I can see the exit signs on the highway so I won't get lost."

Grant began the season still cautious about the change in his eyewear.

"The goggles will take some getting used to," he said. "They're getting knocked off and fogging up sometimes, but it's nice to be able to see so clearly."

The Bulls liked what they saw of Grant in training camp. Jackson cited his maturity and hard work.

Which shows that a man wearing glasses can be tough off the glass too. – SAM SMITH

PAXSON HELPS BULLS ROLL LUCKY SEVEN

he setting was perfect for a big night from the Bulls' veteran guard: Playing in the home of the stars with celebrities courtside, a national cable TV audience watching and an important victory needed for his team.

So John Paxson stepped center stage and led the Bulls past the Los Angeles Clippers 105-97 Nov.23. It was the beginning of an eventual seven-game winning streak.

Paxson scored 26 points, including 20 in the first half as the Bulls....

Wait a second. How long had this West Coast road trip lasted? Is anyone hallucinating? Sure that wasn't Michael Jordan?

No, Jordan totaled just 14 points, matching a three-year career low.

Paxson, coming up just one short of his career high, had 12 baskets in a team-high 16 attempts.

"They made the commitment early to double-team Michael with my man, so he was kicking the ball out and I made my shots early," said Paxson, who was called "Jim"—his brother's name—on the postgame report by the local TV broadcasters.

"After that, Scottie [Pippen] was real unselfish on the break and looking for me.

"We've talked about distributing the ball and getting it to different guys, and this was a real unselfish game from a lot of guys."

Namely Pippen, who picked up his second career triple-double with 13 points, 13 rebounds and 12 assists.

"I had been struggling," said Pippen, shooting just 42 percent on the season. "I was trying to find a way to break through, so I got on the boards, like I've been able to do in the past, and helped get the break going."

As for Jordan, he picked up his second game of 14 points in the last five and was mostly another guy out there.

"I guess if it came down to it, he [Jackson] could have run me into the post and let me use my height and strength to beat [Gary] Grant. But we were getting things easily with me being a decoy. So we were going to the open man, and I was trying to fit into the style of play."

That style was equal opportunity at its best, as the Bulls' starters all took between eight and 16 shots and Dennis Hopson came off the bench to tie a season-high with 13.

They bolted out behind Paxson in the first quarter, going on an 18-4 run, with Paxson supplying 10 of those points on the way to 14 for the quarter.

"I was open. I wasn't thinking, I was just shooting," said Paxson.

Paxson continued his hot ways, drilling three jumpers to begin the second half.

– SAM SMITH

Michael Jordan drives on Pacers' Reggie Miller during the Bulls 124-95 November win.
PHOTO BY CHARLES CHERNEY

The Bulls stumbled out of the blocks with the weight of high expectations before B.J. Armstrong got his first look at crunch time—and the Bulls got their first look at the win column Nov. 7. Armstrong scored 12 of his 14 points in the second half in a 96-91 road win over Minnesota to snap a three-game losing streak. Then the Bulls put together a different streak—this time, winning—at the end of November, beating Indiana by 29 points on the final day of the month. Michael Jordan scored 37 points, 20 in the first quarter.

DECE

'Tis the season to be jostling—with the Pistons. The Bulls renewed a rivalry that lacked the usual holiday greetings, though there was plenty of

PHOTO BY BOB LANGER

good cheer in Chicago Stadium on Christmas Day. The feast started early in the month, with a plentiful first quarter against Cleveland.

MBER

WINS & LOSSES

11-3

ENDING IT EARLY

ortunately for the Cleveland Cavaliers, they don't play the Harlem Globetrotters this season. After the Bulls toyed with Cleveland on Dec. 15 at the Stadium with a first-quarter performance that went down in the Chicago record book, the injury-plagued Cavs could empathize with the Globetrotters' many victims.

The Bulls scored 26 consecutive points, a team record, in the first quarter of their second blowout in as many nights. They built a 36-5 lead and went on to win 116-98.

The five points scored by the Cavs in the first quarter set another Bulls record for fewest points allowed in a quarter.

"Wasn't that something?" Bulls coach Phil Jackson marveled. "I think everyone wanted to go home after that and ask, 'Why play the [rest of the] game?'"

Michael Jordan led the Bulls with 24 points in 27 minutes, adding five of his team's 12 steals. Jordan had 10 points in the wild first quarter, including three of the Bulls' six slams during the period.

The Cavs shot a pitiful 11.1 percent to the Bulls' 69.6 percent in the first quarter.

"The philosophy in this league," Bill Cartwright said, "is beat 'em as bad as they can be beat."

Cleveland finally reached double digits with 9:40 left in the half when Steve Kerr's three-pointer made the score 40-12. They outscored the Bulls in each of the last three quarters to stave off total embarrassment, but Jackson sat Jordan, Cartwright and Grant for most of the second and all of the fourth quarter.

Did Jordan get bored on the bench?

"Bored? No," he said. "I think we need to play more of these games." – PAUL SULLIVAN

The Stadium scoreboard tells the story during the Bulls' record-setting, first-quarter performance versus Cleveland.
PHOTO BY CHARLES CHERNEY

Even in December, Michael Jordan soared higher than Vlade Divac and the rest of the Lakers. PHOTO BY ED WAGNER

On Dec. 21, the first regular-season matchup with the Lakers, the Bulls weren't too concerned with foreshadowing. They just wanted a win, having lost to Detroit two nights earlier. And with all five starters scoring in double figures, they got one, beating L.A. 114-103 in Chicago.

Michael Jordan? A young fan prefers this flying man Christmas Day at the Stadium.
PHOTO BY CHARLES CHERNEY

Peace on Earth? Maybe in some quarters, but Christmas at the Stadium featured the usual combat that goes with a Bulls-Pistons game. The Bulls wanted to avenge a 105-84 loss Dec. 19. "Phil [Jackson] talked with us about playing more physical," John Paxson said. "It's one thing to talk about it and another to do it on the floor." Paxson scored 15 points, second to Michael Jordan's 37, but physical defense keyed the 98-86 win.

Jordan drives on Joe Dumars during the Bulls' Christmas present to themselves—a 12-point win over the rival Pistons.
PHOTO BY CHARLES CHERNEY

DUELING WITH DETROIT

t began with the highest hopes for the Chicago Bulls organization since the mid-'70s and ended with a migraine, of all things. And somehow, it seemed to figure. For the Chicago-Detroit playoff rivalry between 1988 and 1990 was as much a testimony to the

determination and improvement of the Bulls as it was a colossal headache.

After watching Chicago lose by 19 points to the Pistons in the seventh and deciding game of the 1990 NBA Eastern Conference finals—a game in which Scottie Pippen's migraine contributed to his 1 for 10 shooting—General Manager Jerry Krause could take it no longer. All 5 feet 7 inches of him burst into his team's dressing room and all but took a door off its hinges.

By Melissa Isaacson and Paul Sullivan

"I think they saw me madder than I've ever been," he says. "I told them I wasn't mad at them. I never accused them of anything or knocked them. I was just mad at giving those speeches after every year: 'We'll be better next year.'

"I said: 'I don't want to talk to you guys at the end of next year. I want to celebrate.' I got very emotional. Some things were kicked. They understood that I wanted to win badly, or worse. I was embarrassed."

It sure didn't start that way.

The 1987-88 season, the second under coach Doug Collins, ended with the Bulls having won 50 games and losing 32, the franchise's best record since 1974-75 and an improvement over a 30-52 mark two years before.

It was the rookie year of Scottie Pippen and Horace Grant; the last for Charles Oakley, Sedale Threatt, Rory Sparrow and Granville Waiters.

The Bulls won seven of their first eight games and finished second in the Central Division.

In May, the Bulls won a playoff series for the first

time since 1981.

In their first playoff game against Cleveland, Michael Jordan scored 50 points as the Bulls broke a seven-game playoff losing streak. In Game 2, he had 55.

When the Cavs came back to win Game 3 at home, the Tribune headline read: "Cavs bring Bulls back to earth . . . Limit Jordan to 38 points."

"We can win when I don't score 50 points," Jordan said defiantly. But the Bulls lost Game 4 with Jordan scoring 44. Maybe the Bulls couldn't win with Jordan scoring below 50.

Then the world discovered Pippen.

Carrying a 7.9-point average into the playoffs, he picked an opportune time to come of age. He scored 24 points in Game 5 to Jordan's 39 and displayed a flair with which Bulls fans soon would become familiar.

More happy times would come only after three straight years of ending their season with a loss to Detroit.

The 1988-89 season was to be a turning point in the franchise's history. The Bulls enjoyed a 32-20 record until Feb. 24, 1989, but played .500 ball over their final 30 games to finish fifth, setting up a first-round rematch with Cleveland.

The teams split the first two games of the best-of-five series in Cleveland. Jordan's 44 points in Chicago gave the Bulls a Game 3 victory and a shot to clinch the series at home, but in the 108-105 overtime loss in Game 4, Jordan missed a key free throw in the final seconds of regulation that could have sealed a win.

In Game 5, his buzzer-beating 15-foot jumper over Craig Ehlo at the foul line gave the Bulls a one-point victory and new life in the playoffs.

The momentum of the last-second victory carried over to the next series, where the Bulls upset the Knicks in six games to reach the conference finals for the first time since 1975. Their opponents? The Bad Boys, again.

The Bulls shocked the defending conference champions in Game 1, 94-88. They eventually went home with a split and felt confident the Pistons could be had. In Game 3, the Bulls trailed by eight points with four minutes left before Jordan scored 12 of their last 16 points—including the game-winning, 8-foot bank shot with three seconds left—to put the Bulls up 2-1.

But just when things looked brightest, the Bulls' playoff roller-coaster took one last plunge. They lost the next two games to come home trailing 3-2. And with the pressure on, the Bulls went down without much of a fight, 103-94.

"I think we humbled them a little," said Jordan. "We gave them a dogfight, and turned them into nice guys."

The future would prove otherwise.

The big question after the '88-'89 season was whether the Bulls would draft a point guard or keep Jordan in the demanding role. On draft day, the Bulls chose Iowa point guard B.J. Armstrong in the first round (after making Oklahoma center Stacey King their first pick, sixth overall).

But the stunner occurred less than two weeks after the draft, when the Bulls fired Collins as head coach, replacing him with Jackson.

"When Jerry [Reinsdorf] and I sat down and discussed it," Krause said, "we knew that we were going to get ripped badly."

Jackson, an assistant under Collins, guided the Bulls to a 55-27 record in 1989-90, good for second to Detroit in the division. Pippen continued to improve, making his first All-Star Game. Jordan remained spectacular, scoring a career-high 69 points March 28 in Cleveland.

After disposing of Milwaukee and Philadelphia in the first two rounds of the playoffs, the Bulls set up Round 3 with defending NBA champion Detroit.

Each team held serve on its home floor the first six games of the conference finals. Any nice feeling left from the series the previous year was gone. After a

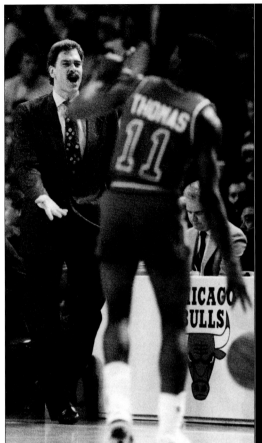

'The thing we really didn't have a grasp of before Phil was how to respond to Detroit's aggressive nature.'
—John Paxson

Phil Jackson barks orders during a Pistons game.
PHOTO BY
ED WAGNER

Game 5 loss to Detroit, Pippen was fined $2,000 for fouling Laimbeer, grabbing him around the neck and slamming him to the floor as he drove to the basket.

After the Bulls trounced the Pistons 109-91 in Game 6, they seemed to have the momentum on their side going into Game 7. But Pippen's migraine, John Paxson's sprained ankle and a woefully low .311 field-goal percentage led to the Bulls' 19-point demise.

"When we went to Detroit for the seventh game, I didn't think we were going to win," Reinsdorf said. "I could see it in the eyes of the players. But it was a very important experience. And in the clubhouse afterward, I really became convinced we were going to win it the next year."

Krause's door-kicking rage helped pound those thoughts home.

"We understood," Paxson said. "The gist of his message was that he never wanted to have to make that speech again. This year, he didn't have to. In all reality, we had to beat that Pistons team to make it worthwhile this year." ■

JANU

One milestone, one millstone. Michael Jordan scored his 15,000th NBA point in Philadelphia. He did it faster than any player but the

legendary Wilt Chamberlain, who played most of his career in Philadelphia. Meanwhile, NBA officials elbowed in on Bill Cartwright's inside moves,

ARY

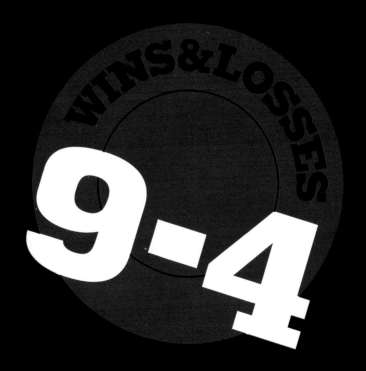

WINS&LOSSES

9-4

PHILADELPHIA–They rose to cheer almost as one, Wednesday night, Jan. 9, and they wouldn't stop. They hooted and howled and clapped–and nobody was even injured.

This is a tough town, Philadelphia. They say the people here will boo a funeral, that it's the people who have to be caged at the zoo.

But when the Bulls' Michael Jordan converted a free throw late in the first quarter for the 15,000th point of his career, more than 18,000 hardened 76ers fans celebrated with an extended standing ovation that Jordan conceded gave him chills. –SAM SMITH, CHICAGO TRIBUNE

PHOTO BY ED WAGNER

'**I**t was a
great feeling to hear that
on the road. When you see
the people respect you like
that, it inspires you to
play well.'

— Michael Jordan

January may have been the cruelest month for the Pistons' Isiah Thomas and the Bulls' Scottie Pippen. Thomas was told Jan. 29 that surgery on his right wrist might keep him out for the season. He would return to appear in 13 playoff games. The same day, Pippen learned that he had not made the NBA Eastern Conference All-Star team. "I'm not disappointed," said Pippen, an All-Star in 1989-90. "I did all I could as a player." Despite his remarks, Pippen was disappointed. He had said a player wasn't established without making the All-Star team more than once. "We just hope [Pippen] doesn't take offense and uses the time off to rest and help improve his team," coach Phil Jackson said.

Scottie Pippen's play rose this season, but he wasn't an All-Star.
PHOTO BY CHARLES CHERNEY

Michael Jordan, in the middle of a Cleveland win, made January a good month.
PHOTO BY ED WAGNER

POINTED CRITICISM FOR CARTWRIGHT

 he National Basketball Association threw a procedural elbow at center Bill Cartwright in January, but Cartwright ducked the blow.

NBA vice president Rod Thorn asked Cartwright to wear elbow pads to avoid potential injuries like the blow to Hakeem Olajuwon's face earlier in the month that resulted in surgery for the Houston center.

Thorn said he did not consider the Olajuwon case an intentional act by Cartwright. Nor, he said, were recent incidents when Jack Sikma had his nose bloodied in a collision with Cartwright and when Greg Kite received stitches to his chin.

But Thorn said: "The blows to the face cannot continue. He has not been fined, as of this time, but whether they were on purpose or not, that is too many blows to the face."

Thorn declined to say if the league had ordered Cartwright to wear elbow pads to protect other players, but Cartwright confirmed he was asked to do so.

"I told him I'd give it all the consideration it deserved," Cartwright said.

Thorn said the league may become more forceful.

"We ask players who are injured and wearing a cast to wear some protection to avoid hurting other players," Thorn said. "We ask them and then we tell them. He has not been told."

The Bulls were prepared to fight any such order.

"It's something we could ask to take to arbitration," said Bulls coach Phil Jackson. "I talked to Bill and asked him if he would feel comfortable [wearing elbow pads] and he said, 'Not at all.' And as soon as he said that, that's my clue to say, 'This guy doesn't feel he can shoot the ball or play with elbow pads, and I don't think he should have to do it.'

"I don't like the attention being drawn to him, because immediately it means the red flag goes up around all his activity."

The Bulls could not afford to have Cartwright limited.

At the time of the incident, he was averaging 10.5 points and 7.4 rebounds in about 30 minutes a game. He also had held opposing starting centers to just over 10 points a game. Cartwright's defense has long been one of his strengths, and the Bulls could ill-afford to have his physical nature hampered.

Cartwright was moving as well as he had before his first foot injury in 1984. Jackson called on him to play additional minutes with the erratic play of backup centers Stacey King and Will Perdue.

Cartwright, 33, who seemed to have slowed, proved almost irreplaceable. He averaged 33 minutes per game in one 16-game stretch, including seven games of at least 35 minutes. In that span, he averaged 12.4 points and eight rebounds.

Never has the league determined that Cartwright deliberately threw an elbow or tried to injure anyone. Two seasons ago, he was fined for several incidents involving elbowing, but the fine was rescinded.

Thorn said no team official had shown him proof during the 1990-91 season of any ill intent on Cartwright's part. However, Thorn admitted he had received complaints.

Jackson said opposing players bring injuries on themselves by playing Cartwright differently.

"A lot of players crowd Bill," Jackson said. "I don't see them crowding [Patrick] Ewing or Olajuwon like that.

"I think the perception is that the guy goes out of his way to knock people down, which is not the case. He establishes position. He will fight for position like any center in the NBA, for he's highly competitive, so he's not going to give ground, and rightly so."

–SAM SMITH

As the Knicks' Charles Oakley learned, Bill Cartwright's elbows can grab their share of attention around the NBA.
PHOTO BY ED WAGNER

FEBR

At the All-Star break, the Bulls stood 32-14. The biggest win of the first half? The Bulls' first regular-season victory ever at the Palace on Feb. 7. It proved inspirational; the Bulls didn't lose again this month. Tribune readers also made some inspired picks for an all-time Bulls team.

UARY

WINS&LOSSES

11-1

CHET WALKER
Forward: Always a clutch player, Walker is the 19th leading scorer in NBA history.
PHOTO BY ED WAGNER

BOB LOVE
Forward: "Butterbean" led the Bulls in scoring for seven straight seasons in the '70s.
PHOTO BY ED WAGNER

MICHAEL JORDAN
Guard: A two-time league MVP, Jordan already is the Bulls' all-time leader in scoring.
PHOTO BY JOHN KUNTZ

To commemorate the Bulls' 25th anniversary season, the Tribune asked its readers to select an all-time Bulls team. Above are the winners, while Norm Van Lier, John Paxson, Tom Boerwinkle, Horace Grant and Scottie Pippen made second team.

JERRY SLOAN
Guard: Sloan is the all-time leader in games and the only Bull to have his jersey retired.
PHOTO BY FRANK HANES

ARTIS GILMORE
Center: The "A Train" is the Bulls' and NBA's all-time leader in field goal percentage.
PHOTO BY ED WAGNER

RED-HOT HODGES

This season wasn't fun for guard Craig Hodges, relegated mostly to mopup duty.

He played 11.5 minutes a game while shooting 42.4 percent, lowest on the team.

But for one night, at least, Craig Hodges proved what he believes he is.

"I feel at this moment that I'm the best shooter on planet Earth," Hodges said, caressing the trophy for winning the NBA's long-distance shooting contest.

No one disputed him, not even Larry Bird, long considered the best three-point shooter in NBA history.

"Like Sugar Ray Leonard says," Hodges challenged, "if he wants to come out of [tournament shooting] retirement, I'm here."

"Here" was atop the shooting world.

Hodges shattered all of Bird's records in winning the shooting contest, held as a preliminary to the All-Star Game.

Hodges did it in such style that he drew a standing ovation from All-Stars Magic Johnson, Dominique Wilkins, Joe Dumars and Kevin Johnson, who witnessed the exhibition Feb. 9 with more than 23,000 fans in Charlotte, N.C.

Hodges, winning his second straight three-point shooting title, hit 19 straight at one point, a run that brought the roaring crowd to its feet, counting along with each shot until the 20th spun out.

"I thought I could make every shot," Hodges said. "I've been on great rolls before, but never when the popcorn was popping and the people were in the stands." – SAM SMITH

FREEZE FRAME

Bernie Lincicome

IN THE WAKE
OF THE NEWS

Geography is one thing. The calendar is another.

Heading into March as the best team in the East is not quite the same as doing it in June when there are championship banners to be unwrinkled for the Stadium's empty rafters.

Routing the Boston Celtics at the end of February is not the same as doing it at the end of May.

Or on the road. Or when Kevin McHale is working on both ankles and Larry Bird isn't stoved up like an ironing board.

"I think the Bulls treated this game like it was the playoffs," said Boston coach Chris Ford.

Well, the Bulls are still new at this bully business and will apparently take with both hands whatever there is to be had and worry about what it all means later.

The Bulls ought to give Tuesday night's merry romp over Boston to a competent cryogenicist, one of the fast-freeze guys, who can thaw it out later when it is really needed.

That way you can be sure that Scottie Pippen is as alert and accurate, as determinedly arrogant as he appears to be, flying into danger or over it.

That Cliff Levingston, if needed again in relief of Horace Grant, gone with a bum ankle six minutes into the game, will be a help and not a hindrance.

Or Will Perdue will enter the game to encouraging cheers, not anxious to hurt either himself or his friends.

And Michael Jordan, of course, remaining Michael Jordan for as long as it takes.

You do not beat the Celtics by 30 every night, or every decade for that matter. At least I assume those were the Celtics. They wore green shirts and black shoes and played one half of the court at a time.

Who or whatever they were played like refrigerator magnets. ■

John Paxson, Will Perdue and Bill Cartwright suffer yet another disappointment at the Palace in Detroit.
PHOTO BY CHARLES CHERNEY

'The Bulls are the best team I've ever seen. Go ahead, write that. Maybe it will put some pressure on them.'
– Larry Bird

**Will Perdue helped give the Celtics a bird's-eye view of a blowout in February.
PHOTO BY ED WAGNER**

It seemed like forever–and it was. The Bulls had never notched a regular-season win in the Palace of Auburn Hills until the night of Feb. 7. Then, riding a Michael Jordan stretch run, the Bulls ended the Palace jinx with a 95-93 come-from-behind win, outscoring Detroit 10-4 in the final 2:13. "This was great for our confidence and the mental aspect of knowing we can beat this team on other than our home court," said Jordan, who scored the final 10 Bulls' points to finish with 30.

MARC

While Indiana's Reggie Miller became too noticeable for his own team's good, Chicago's unsung heroes Scottie Pippen and Horace Grant merely continued to clean the glass. The Bulls, angling for home court advantage in the playoffs, mopped up Eastern Conference foes.

PHOTO BY CHARLES CHERNEY

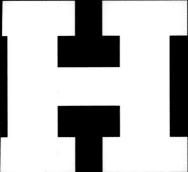

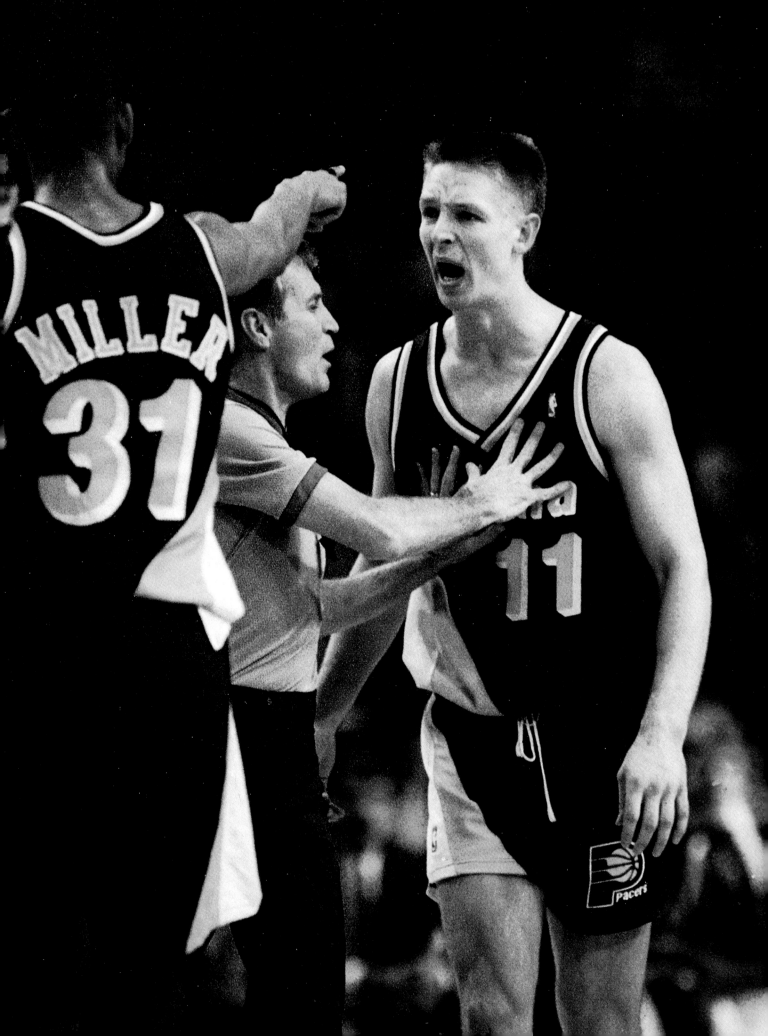

BULLS 'NOBODIES' FIND SOMEBODY TO BEAT

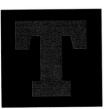he words stung.

"Take Michael Jordan off their team and who do they have? Nobody. Michael Jordan makes the team."

The speaker was Reggie Miller of the Pacers, and he spoke on March 2 in Indianapolis from the high ground of the winner's locker room.

The Bulls had lost to Miller's team 135-114.

His remark was a curious one because Jordan had played almost to the end and had scored 22 points. The man the Bulls really missed was Horace Grant, out with a sprained ankle.

Without his speed, the Bulls had trouble beating the Pacers down the floor.

Still the words hurt. Nobodies.

The Bulls soon got their revenge. With Miller's remark pasted up in their locker room, the Bulls went after the Pacers March 23 at the Stadium, where the fans chanted obscenities at Miller and booed him every time he touched the ball.

Jordan scored 39 points, but John Paxson, one of the nobodies, added 25 in the 133-119 victory.

The talk continued well into the game.

"You could say they lost their poise," Jordan said. "The things said before and during the game got everyone going, and I think some statements were made."

The Bulls' vengeful win is too much for Detlef Schrempf, who was ejected.
PHOTO BY JIM PRISCHING

The Pacers' Detlef Schrempf was ejected in the first half after tangling with a Bill Cartwright elbow. Then Chuck Person got the thumb in the fourth quarter after he kicked the basketball nearly into the first balcony. Person's tantrum came after a foul and near fight with Will Perdue.

Miller, at least, backed up his talk with 34 points.

"It was some shootout," coach Phil Jackson said. "But I think these guys felt insulted and the team felt maligned in its own way that a professional would say something like that to denigrate their talents.

"Miller had a great game, but it was not up to Michael Jordan's standards."

The victory was the Bulls' 26th straight at home and it put them a game closer to clinching their division. The Pacers, 34-35 at the time, were in line to be the Bulls' first-round opponent.

"[The Bulls] definitely don't want us in the playoffs," Person challenged. "We can beat the Bulls and they know it."

More talk.

"They're a real cocky team that talks a lot of trash," Scottie Pippen said. "For us to be in a position that we're in, we feel we should beat that type of team. So it became a very emotional game."

Paxson allowed that the Pacers were "a very good team."

"They played the second half without Schrempf and then Person gets kicked out," he said. "And they played us tough."

But Jordan summed up the Bulls' approach to the game and the season.

"We maintained our poise and let our basketball do the talking," he said. –SAM SMITH

ome court in the playoffs goes to the conference leaders. In the NBA East, that was the Bulls as March ended. "We control our destiny," Michael Jordan said.

APRIL

And now, introducing a host of regular-season achievements for "your Chicago Bulls"... a Central Division title, the best record in the Eastern Conference, a franchise-high 61 victories, an all-time home win streak. Also, we present a lightning-fast defense that provides quick offense.

PHOTO BY MILBERT ORLANDO BROWN

WINS&LOSSES

8-3

IN THE SPOTLIGHT

To some, it's merely hype. But, for many, including the Bulls, it offers hope. "Do you know when it helps the most?" asked Bill Cartwright. "If you ever come to the game lacking energy. The introduction, and that noise, gets it back for you." It starts with darkness, then music and spotlights fill the air. Then, public address announcer Ray Clay's voice, booming, over the Stadium loudspeaker: "And now, the starting lineup for your Chicago Bulls . . ." Cheers follow, along with a rush that is different for each individual player. "It gives me chills every time," said Michael Jordan. The warmth of the spotlight grabs each player, but so does the thrill of hearing 18,000 fans scream their affection during an introduction unmatched in sports.

Before every home game, the Bulls starting lineup is announced in a theatrical fashion with music, spotlights and noise. PHOTOS BY CHARLES CHERNEY (RIGHT) AND ED WAGNER

A capacity crowd of 18,676 fills the Chicago Stadium each time the Bulls play a home game. PHOTO BY EDUARDO CONTRERAS

HOME SWEET HOME

Instead of a Kansas twister, the Bulls had to survive whirlwind performances from the likes of David Robinson, Karl Malone and Charles Barkley. But, like Dorothy, they too found there is no place like home, going 35-6 in the familiar sanctity of the Stadium during the regular season and 8-1 in the playoffs. What's more, in one

Michael Jordan (above) and Bulls' fans are right in the action together.
PHOTOS BY CHARLES CHERNEY (ABOVE) AND ED WAGNER

stretch this season, the Bulls went more than three months without losing a home game. "I love [Chicago Stadium] because everybody hates it," said Michael Jordan. "They think it's old and everything. I think it gives us a good edge. The crowd is right there on the floor. I don't think you're going to find another stadium, or build another stadium, like Chicago Stadium, where every seat has a good view. I love it." The fans, too, seem to love it as the Bulls have sold out 190 consecutive home games and created a home court advantage rivaling any other in sport. "This building is crazy. It's loud. I mean real loud. If there's an arena that's louder, I'd like to know which one it is," said Barkley.

BULLS NEVER LET THEIR DEFENSE REST

n a dimly lit room in the basement of a suburban New York gym where his team practiced, John MacLeod and his New York Knicks coaching staff spent long hours in late April analyzing just how they could overcome the Bulls' most impressive threat. It's one that baffled the

Knicks and, in fact, much of the NBA this past season. Controlling it, the Knicks knew, was the key to defeating the Bulls.

And it wasn't Michael Jordan.

Sure, the Knicks were concerned about Jordan, whom MacLeod has said is the "best to ever play the game."

But it's the Bulls' various and changing defenses, their traps and barely disguised zones, their pressure and their athleticism on defense that has become their most potent weapon. Perhaps more than anything it's responsible for the team's success this past season.

"It's something that's helped us attain the record we have," said Bulls coach Phil Jackson, the primary architect of the defense. "People understand the Bulls are a quick, sure-handed team that gets a lot of steals and a lot of easy baskets. A lot of breakaway things happen positively for us.

"What the defense can do is rattle teams and give us those 10-0 bursts that have become our mark," noted Jackson. "You can jump out and suddenly a team is in a crisis situation."

Indeed, the Bulls did that with amazing regularity this season, as the Knicks surely know. For it was against the Knicks early in April that the Bulls sprang one of their most effective traps, their so-called firemen's drill defense, which is a furious all-court trap. It helped the Bulls bounce back from a 24-point deficit to win going away.

By Sam Smith

"Their defensive intensity has picked up this season," said Pistons assistant and chief advance scout Brendan Malone. "They're probably the best pressing team in the league."

And, certainly, it's Jordan who helps assure that with his quickness and ability to steal the ball. But no more than Scottie Pippen, also a key figure when the Bulls spring a trap.

"Michael and Scottie are outstanding stealers," said assistant John Bach, who built the defenses from Jackson's ideas.

But perhaps no player is more important to the Bulls' defensive schemes—and whose improvement enabled it to develop—than Horace Grant.

"He's the intrepid one," said Bach. "He goes the full 94 feet. He's the one who has to meet the point of the ball on the double-team and then sometimes a second time as he goes down court. And then he has to find a man to guard and rebound.

"He's the one who's really helped the press more than anyone else. We've always had the ability to run/jump trap (trapping the ballhandler with two guards), but he's given us the addition of a big man able to do that.

"So now you've got Pippen at about 6-8 and Horace at 6-10 and Michael at 6-6—but who plays much bigger—and they're roaring around the court in a triangle of defenders and interceptors anchored by stability in the guard position in John Paxson and Bill Cartwright in the back. It's something that requires long preparation against this team."

The philosophy behind the Bulls' defense comes from Jackson's experience as a player with the Knicks and the influences of his college coach, Bill Fitch, and former Knicks coach Hubie Brown.

Good defense has never been underestimated in the NBA. It both upsets the plan of an offense and leads to fast breaks in transition, which is vital to the Bulls, a team without a dominating post player. Jackson also likes the idea that it unites the players in a concept without the ball in producing a sense of teamwork.

"I remember when Red Holzman took over in my first year with the Knicks and the first day of practice," Jackson recalls. "He called a '10' defense, which was full-court pressure. He threw the ball in, and we picked up a man, and the Knicks played full-court pressure until about 1972, when we started to get older and had less and less speed.

"Basically, defense is hard work and labor," noted Jackson. "Guys on the ball side taking away the passing lanes and guys on the back side two passes away helping. The basic idea is vision of what the offense is trying to execute, vision of the ball and defensively touching the man."

But it's also a belief in what the players can do and a willingness by the coach to accept the inevitable breakdowns. Defense the way the Bulls often play it can be a risk.

"Our defense is a mixture," Bach said. "It has all kinds of ingredients that take advantage of the slashing and quick-hands ability of our players. But it's the boldness of Phil in his calls and his patience when it doesn't succeed that makes it work for this team."

Since it's freshest in the minds of the Knicks—and worked effectively in the playoffs last season when the Bulls almost overcame a 24-point deficit against the 76ers—it may be best to start with the firemen's drill.

It's a helter-skelter, rotate-and-recover press and trap that can throw teams into chaos. Jackson usually calls for a small lineup, and even if it doesn't result in steals, it can force a team to begin its offense in the last 10 seconds of the 24-second clock, thus making decision-making difficult for all but the best teams.

"It's been the most rewarding because Phil has practiced it from Day 1," said Bach. "Initially, the players, and even the coaches, were shaking their heads over the chaos, but they found it shifting to the other teams."

The Bulls practice the firemen's drill as a 12-man game in which four play four. When the defense turns to offense, there's another four-man team waiting for them at the other end of the floor, and the whole sequence of trapping and rushing begins again.

So while it builds reaction to offense for the Bulls, it also trains them against defensive pressure.

The Bulls only call that out in desperate situations, but they probably pick up full court as much as any team in the league.

They are not a full-court pressing team because their lead guards, Paxson and B.J. Armstrong, do not have the quickness to push a guard the whole length of the court. That was one reason the Bulls were looking for a guard like Derek Harper this season. But Paxson is effective.

"He really picks up better than he has any right to," Bach said.

The Bulls are most likely to pressure full court after made free throws, new quarters or timeouts— times they have a chance to set up.

One of their typical presses is their "Dallas" call, on which Paxson applies some pressure to the guard getting the ball. That pass is usually allowed. But then Grant jumps in to try to block vision and obscure a pass while Cartwright comes up and Jordan and Pippen drop into the passing lanes. Again, the most responsibility is left to Grant because his man is usually the one who has inbounded the ball, so he has to try to quick trap and then rush back to meet his man heading upcourt.

Run/jump is another of the Bulls' favorite pressure defenses. This occurs after a guard gets around midcourt.

Although the Bulls do trap full court, they consider themselves a team that plays its best defense in the midcourt area. They do this because they lack the overall guard speed to pressure full court and the big bodies like a Portland or Detroit to hold players out of the lane. And Cartwright provides what the Bulls consider a "front" in the lane that makes players go around because he'll step up and hit someone.

> **'They're probably the best pressing team in the league'**
> **- Pistons assistant and scout Brendan Malone**

Defensively, Scottie Pippen and friends had a hand up on the competition.
PHOTO BY MILBERT ORLANDO BROWN

"Sometimes, they'll try to go over the top," said Jackson, "but they know it won't be comfortable."

In a run/jump, Jordan, playing the other guard, will jump at the ballhandler with Paxson sliding under and hopefully into that passing lane to the player Jordan left. Then Pippen steps up across the court into that passing lane, which gives him those steals for full-court breaks while Cartwright must lay back and "zone" the middle under the basket. Plus, Grant will jump at the

guard to help Jordan, but also must be quick to recover as his man comes down the middle and toward the basket.

It's the combination of those long arms and quick hands that results in so many steals and fast-break baskets for the Bulls.

Generally, the Bulls will try to make the guard zigzag up with the ball because a team never wants an offense to come straight down. Paxson or Armstrong might

also try to harass the point guard to force another player, perhaps not as good in decision-making, to bring the ball up. And the point guards also are charged with forcing the ballhandler to one side so the Bulls can overload against him for the trap rather than allowing him to operate in the middle.

In addition to getting the Bulls into a transition game without a shot-blocker or dominant rebounder, their pressure defense keeps them from having to play against more debilitating screen/roll plays and hard screens that can wear them down. It also transforms their speed and quickness into an instant offense.

But Jackson knows it's hardly flawless. The gambling puts extreme pressure on the backline players like Grant and Cartwright and can be attacked with time.

"It's something that helped us get a good record," Jackson noted, "although I don't know how well we can play it in the playoffs. But I think we can screw it up and use it to our advantage and make some things happen positively for us." ■

SIGNALS OF SUCCESS

Seconds are left in the game and the Bulls players are crouching into their defensive stances.

The Bulls coaches are leaning forward in their seats, watching the opponents' bench. John Paxson is backpedaling slightly, watching both the bench and the point guard who is waiting for the inbounds pass. The game is on the line.

"Savior! Savior!" the visiting bench starts to scream. "Savior!"

"Savior," yells the point guard, which Paxson hears and repeats over his shoulder to his Bulls' teammates,

It's barely audible 10 feet away, but Michael Jordan hears, as does Scottie Pippen.

Jordan's man, they know, will now be curling around a double screen.

Pippen steps in to disrupt the screen and Jordan squeezes through to get to the shooter. The shot is wide and the Bulls win.

There will be no savior for the visitors this night.

But there once was, which resulted in the name for that particular play.

There are many other plays, like "What the hell," and "Soft Blue," "Snake," "Bump" and "Pistol."

And they're all part of the behind-the-scenes science and intelligence-gathering of professional basketball.

Like "UCLA," which has nothing to do with Lakers fans.

"That's probably the most common call in the NBA," said Bulls defensive assistant John Bach.

It represents a series of definitive cuts and actions by an offense and although teams have different names for it, the Bulls use their UCLA call to alert the team.

So the Bulls will identify this action—perhaps known as "Hawk"—to one team. When that call is made, the Bulls' bench and usually the lead guard, either Paxson or Jordan, will call "UCLA," thus alerting

the Bulls players there will be a play with a pass, cut and perhaps a postup screen coming.

This isn't something only the Bulls do. In fact, it's quite common around the NBA. But the Bulls, behind Bach and assistant Jim Cleamons, have made it a major part of their defensive scheme.

The defense starts with what the Bulls like to call recognition, the series of their opponents' signals that match their plays.

Those calls can be as simple as any in baseball or as complex as any in football.

Bach, though, said it still comes down to the effort of your players.

"Defense starts with a determination and pride to excel," Bach said. "It comes with knowledge and communication and you've got to have heart. We like to say, 'To the timid soul nothing is possible. To the aggressor, everything is possible.' " – SAM SMITH

PHOTO BY CHARLES CHERNEY

Bulls regular season results

Home team all caps

Date	Result	Bulls top scorer	Bulls top rebounder
November			
11/2	76ers 124, BULLS 116	Jordan (34)	Levingston (6)
11/3	BULLETS 103, Bulls 102	Jordan (28)	Jordan (10)
11/6	Celtics 110, BULLS 108	Jordan (33)	Cartwright, Jordan (8)
11/7	Bulls 96, WOLVES 91	Jordan, Grant (17)	Grant (10)
11/9	Bulls 120, CELTICS 100	Jordan (41)	Levingston (12)
11/10	BULLS 105, Hornets 86	Jordan (23)	Cartwright (7)
11/13	Bulls 84, JAZZ 82	Jordan (29)	Grant, Jordan (11)
11/15	WARRIORS 103, Bulls 93	Grant (18)	Pippen (9)
11/17	Bulls 116, SONICS 95	Jordan (33)	Pippen (10)
11/18	BLAZERS 125, Bulls 112	Jordan (29)	Cartwright (8)
11/21	SUNS 109, Bulls 107	Jordan (34)	Cartwright (12)
11/23	Bulls 105, CLIPPERS 97	Paxson (26)	Pippen (13)
11/24	Bulls 151, NUGGETS 145	Jordan (38)	Cartwright (8)
11/28	Bulls 118, BULLETS 94	Jordan (24)	Cartwright (8)
11/30	BULLS 124, Pacers 95	Jordan (37)	Grant (9)
December			
12/1	Bulls 120, CAVS 85	Jordan (32)	Cartwright (9)
12/4	BULLS 155, Suns 127	Jordan (27)	Grant (12)
12/7	BULLS 108, Knicks 98	Jordan (33)	Grant (13)
12/8	Blazers 109, BULLS 101	Jordan (35)	Pippen (14)
12/11	BUCKS 99, Bulls 87	Jordan (31)	Grant (9)
12/14	BULLS 128, Clippers 88	Pippen (22)	Perdue (9)
12/15	BULLS 116, Cavs 98	Jordan (24)	Jordan (9)
12/18	BULLS 112, Heat 103	Jordan (39)	Jordan (9)
12/19	PISTONS 105, Bulls 84	Jordan (33)	Grant, Pippen (9)
12/21	BULLS 114, Lakers 103	Jordan (33)	Jordan (15)
12/22	BULLS 128, Pacers 118	Jordan (29)	Pippen, Cartwright (10)
12/25	BULLS 98, Pistons 86	Jordan (37)	Cartwright (10)
12/27	BULLS 128, Warriors 113	Jordan (42)	Jordan (14)
12/29	BULLS 116, Sonics 91	Jordan (31)	Cartwright (13)
January 1991			
1/3	ROCKETS 114, Bulls 92	Jordan (32)	Grant (12)
1/5	BULLS 108, Cavs 92	Jordan (30)	Grant (11)
1/8	Bulls 111, NETS 102	Jordan (41)	Pippen (12)
1/9	Bulls 107, 76ERS 99	Jordan (40)	Grant (10)
1/11	BULLS 99, Hawks 96	Jordan (31)	3 players (10)
1/12	Bulls 106, HORNETS 95	Jordan (33)	Grant, Cartwright (11)
1/14	BULLS 110, Bucks 97	Jordan (34)	Grant (12)
1/16	Bulls 99, MAGIC 88	Jordan (29)	Grant (13)
1/18	HAWKS 114, Bulls 105	Jordan (30)	Grant (10)
1/21	Bulls 117, HEAT 106	Jordan (37)	Grant (10)
1/23	NETS 99, Bulls 95	Jordan (35)	Grant (11)
1/25	BULLS 108, Heat 87	Jordan (26)	Levingston (10)
1/31	SPURS 106, Bulls 102	Jordan (36)	Grant (16)
February			
2/1	Bulls 101, MAVERICKS 90	Jordan (31)	Pippen (14)
2/3	LAKERS 99, Bulls 86	Jordan (23)	Perdue (11)
2/4	Bulls 108, KINGS 97	Jordan (24)	Perdue (14)
2/7	Bulls 95, PISTONS 93	Jordan (30)	Jordan (9)
2/12	BULLS 122, Hawks 113	Jordan (32)	Grant, King (6)
2/14	Bulls 102, KNICKS 92	Jordan (29)	King (9)
2/16	BULLS 99, Nets 87	Jordan (26)	Jordan, Perdue (11)
2/18	Bulls 110, CAVS 95	Jordan (32)	Cartwright (7)
2/19	BULLS 118, Bullets 113	Jordan (40)	Pippen (13)
2/22	BULLS 129, Kings 82	Jordan (34)	Pippen (10)
2/23	BULLS 129, Hornets 108	Pippen (43)	Grant (17)
2/26	BULLS 129, Celtics 99	Jordan (39)	Jordan, Perdue (8)

Fans display their winning attitude during a playoff game.
PHOTO BY ED WAGNER

Date	Result	Bulls top scorer	Bulls top rebounder
March			
3/1	BULLS 109, Mavericks 86	Jordan (29)	Jordan (11)
3/2	PACERS 135, Bulls 114	Jordan (22)	Perdue (13)
3/5	BULLS 104, Bucks 86	Jordan (30)	Pippen (10)
3/8	BULLS 99, Jazz 89	Jordan (37)	Cartwright (9)
3/10	Bulls 122, HAWKS 87	Jordan (25)	Levingston (10)
3/12	BULLS 131, Wolves 99	Jordan, Grant (20)	Grant (12)
3/13	Bulls 102, BUCKS 101	Jordan (39)	Grant (11)
3/15	Bulls 105, HORNETS 92	Jordan (34)	Perdue (12)
3/16	Bulls 102, CAVS 98	Jordan (37)	Jordan (10)
3/18	BULLS 121, Nuggets 108	Jordan (31)	Pippen (11)
3/20	BULLS 129, Hawks 107	Jordan (22)	Grant(10)
3/22	76ERS 95, Bulls 90	Jordan (20)	Grant (10)
3/23	Bulls 133, PACERS 119	Jordan (39)	Perdue (11)
3/25	Rockets 100, BULLS 90	Jordan (34)	Pippen, Grant (12)
3/28	Bulls 128, NETS 94	Jordan (42)	Pippen (14)
3/29	Bulls 112, BULLETS 94	Grant, Pippen (22)	Grant(13)
3/30	CELTICS 135, Bulls 132	Jordan (37)	Grant (18)
April			
4/2	BULLS 106, Magic 102	Jordan (44)	Grant (7)
4/4	Bulls 101, KNICKS 91	Jordan (34)	Pippen (10)
4/5	Spurs 110, BULLS 107	Jordan (39)	Grant (10)
4/7	76ers 114, BULLS 111	Jordan (41)	Grant (7)
4/9	BULLS 108, Knicks 106	Jordan (28)	Grant (14)
4/10	Bulls 101, PACERS 96	Jordan (28)	Grant (7)
4/12	PISTONS 95, Bulls 91	Jordan (40)	Pippen (11)
4/15	BULLS 103, Bucks 94	Jordan (46)	Grant (11)
4/17	Bulls 111, HEAT 101	Jordan (26)	Pippen (11)
4/19	Bulls 115, HORNETS 99	Jordan (41)	Grant (11)
4/21	BULLS 108, Pistons 100	Pippen (28)	Perdue (10)

PLAYO

Easy goes the Eastern Conference. First, the Bulls nicked and cut up New York. Then, they thumped and bumped Charles Barkley and the Sixers. And, in the

PHOTO BY MICHAEL FRYER

sweetest of sweeps, the once-fearsome Pistons were put away in four straight bites. Piece of cake.

OFFS

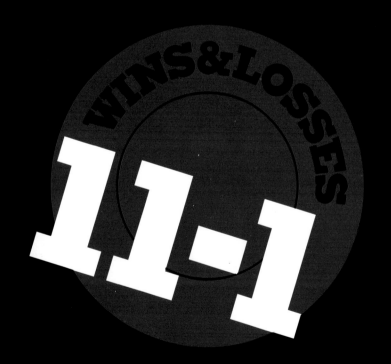

WINS&LOSSES
11-1

BULLS' TIME IS NOW

Bernie Lincicome

IN THE WAKE OF THE NEWS

No excuses.

That's not to say that the Bulls won't have to come up with some before this is all over, but going into the NBA playoffs, what's expected is a coronation.

The Bulls are ripe enough, fit enough and hungry enough.

This is finally the year of the Bull. (Actually, on the Chinese calendar it's the Year of the Goat, but if they were checking IDs at the zoo, Benny the Bull could pass.)

As Jerry Krause, the antsy architect of whatever happens between now and the middle of June, was saying, "Everything we've done for the last six years has been designed to win the World Championship."

That would include, as I recall, changing coaches every other year, drafting and abandoning incomplete curiosities, and, most importantly, doing nothing to disgust Michael Jordan into taking up golf full time.

A good sports administrator has to have a plan.

The toughest thing the Bulls will have to do is leap over the invalids littering the way to the finals.

Isiah Thomas has one hand, Larry Bird has a bum back and Charles Barkley can only use one leg at a time.

The path to glory is paved with another team's bandages.

The Bulls need 11 victories to get to the NBA Finals, which ought to come without more than four losses spaced without real peril along the way.

On the other side, I figure it will be the Lakers for no other reason than I want it to be. I want to see Magic Johnson playing Jordan for everything before it's too late for one or both of them. Then, I'll take Jordan in six. **(APRIL 25, 1991)**

The Knicks were as lifeless as the Bulls were buoyant in the three-game sweep.
PHOTO BY CHARLES CHERNEY

New York Gets the Point

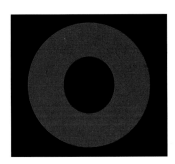

One word summed up the first round of the playoffs for the Bulls: Sweep!

Note the exclamation point. The Bulls' three straight wins over the New York Knicks on April 25, 28 and 30 were like a whoop, a cheer and a shout, announcing that this team could be a force in games to come.

They started it with two victories in the Stadium, a 126-85 slamming and an 89-79 defensive gem. The Bulls punctuated it with a 103-94 victory in New York, clinching the best-of-five series.

"This ballclub was determined to go through the Knicks and not let anything unnatural happen, like an upset," coach Phil Jackson said.

By Sam Smith

The Bulls, in overwhelming the Knicks in Game 1, played like a whole team of naturals.

Michael Jordan led the way with 28 points. Scottie Pippen added 25 points and four steals while the Bulls exasperated and devastated the Knicks in running up a team-record playoff victory margin of 41 points, 14 more than the old mark.

"They were very aware of our defense," Jordan said. "It was like they were looking over their shoulders and our defense kept coming and they got real loose with the ball. It seemed liked the pressure started getting to them."

Patrick Ewing, the Knicks' center and leading scorer, played like a drowning man who was thrown a lead weight by Bill Cartwright. Ewing was held to six points, his lowest total in more than 200 games. He was in foul trouble much of the way.

Bill Cartwright battles Knicks' center Patrick Ewing. Photo By Ed Wagner

The Bulls' bench, led by B.J. Armstrong with a personal playoff high of 18 points and Craig Hodges with 16, looked like a million dollars.

In Game 2, the Knicks managed to lift themselves from footwipe to nuisance, causing some concern about Game 3.

"This team," Jackson said of his Bulls, "is not interested in playing any more games than it has to."

As it turned out, the Knicks did improve in Game 3—by one, from a 10- point loss in Game 2 to a nine-pointer.

"It was a great game by Michael Jordan [33 points, six steals] and Scottie Pippen [21 points, 11 rebounds, four steals]," Jackson said of the clincher. "And great relief help from Will Perdue [16 points, 10 rebounds]."

Jordan and Pippen placed their own unique exclamation points on the game in the second quarter after the Knicks had taken a 12-point lead.

First, Pippen blew down the lane and slammed over Ewing.

"It was a point to make that we were going to take the ball to the hole," Pippen said.

Then Jordan spun right along the baseline against two defenders and rose above Ewing for another jam. Eleven of the Bulls' 12 second-quarter baskets and 27 of 43 for the game were layups or slams.

The message was sent: We'll take on your best and beat him. Next in line to receive it were the Philadelphia 76ers. ■

TEACHING A LESSON

Composite box: Bulls vs. Knicks

BULLS (3-0)	G	Avg min	FG pct	FT pct	Reb	Ast	Avg pts
Jordan	3	37.6	.525	.956	14	18	29.0
Pippen	3	40	.500	.706	26	15	19.7
Grant	3	39	.461	.786	22	8	11.7
Cartwright	3	26.6	.562	1.000	7	2	8.3
Paxson	3	26.3	.360	1.000	4	8	7.3
Armstrong	3	21.6	.562	.900	6	13	9.3
King	3	11.3	.300	.571	12	0	3.3
Perdue	3	14	.533	.600	12	0	7.3
Hodges	3	13.6	.562	.000	1	0	7.0
Levingston	3	5.6	.667	.000	5	2	1.3
Hopson	3	2.3	.333	.000	1	1	0.7
Williams	3	1.6	.500	.500	3	0	1.0
Totals	**3**	–	**.494**	**.783**	**113**	**67**	**106**

Three-point goals: 8-16, .500 (Jordan 3-6, Hodges 3-5, Armstrong 1-1, Pippen 1-2, Paxson 0-2). **Team rebounds:** 27. **Blocked shots:** 9. **Turnovers:** 37. **Steals:** 37. **Technical fouls:** None. **Illegal defense:** 1. **Flagrant fouls:** None.

KNICKS (0-3)	G	Avg min	FG pct	FT pct	Reb	Ast	Avg pts
Oakley	3	33.3	.476	.500	31	3	7.6
Vandeweghe	3	33	.406	.880	8	4	17
Ewing	3	36.6	.400	.777	30	6	16.6
Cheeks	3	33.6	.609	.500	9	16	10
Tucker	3	22	.360	1.000	12	9	8
G. Wilkins	3	26	.368	1.000	8	5	10.6
Jackson	3	12	.333	.000	0	8	0.6
Walker	3	10.3	.500	1.000	7	2	3.3
Quinnett	3	12	.500	.000	1	3	3
Starks	3	9.3	.400	1.000	3	6	2
E. Wilkins	3	4.3	.667	.500	2	0	3
Mustaf	3	7.3	.800	.800	5	0	4
Totals	**3**	–	**.443**	**.803**	**116**	**62**	**86**

Three-point goals: 11-28, .393 (Vandeweghe 3-5, Tucker 4-10, G. Wilkins 2-7, Quinnett 1-3, Cheeks 1-3). **Team rebounds:** 19. **Blocked shots:** 11. **Turnovers:** 66 . **Steals:** 16. **Technical fouls:** 3. **Illegal defense:** 1. **Flagrant fouls:** 1.

For three seasons in New York, Bill Cartwright was the teacher and Patrick Ewing the pupil. In the Bulls' playoff series against the Knicks, it was obvious that teacher still knew best. Discounting Ewing's rookie year in 1985-86, when injuries forced Cartwright to miss all but two games, the two 7-footers banged against each other in practice for the better part of two seasons. Cartwright, the thinking goes, became familiar with where Ewing liked to maneuver and forced him into spots farther from the basket. "I'm tired of hearing that stuff," Ewing said after Game 1 of this playoff series. "Bill is an outstanding player, but..." But statistics don't lie and Ewing, a 51 percent shooter during the regular season, converted just 40 percent of his shots during the three-game sweep. And in Game 1, Ewing scored just six points, his lowest total in some 200 games. "Patrick had to work so hard to get his shots," said Bulls coach Phil Jackson, "that he kind of wore down."

Chicago Tribune
Sports

Section 4　★　　　　　Wednesday, May 1, 1991

Corporate types go to bat for ghetto youngsters

Near North Little League volunteers, including Rich Adams (second from right) and Bill Harrington (right), with two young ballplayers.
Tribune photo by Jim Prisching

By Steve Hymon
Special to the Tribune

In his 17 years of working with black youths in the Cabrini-Green housing projects, Al Carter has seen some strange things.

But nothing quite like this stranger.

When Carter's revamped African American Youth Baseball League—now being called the Near North Little League—takes the field May 19, teams will bear the names of corporate sponsors and African tribes. The results are such teams as the Ernst & Young Fanti, Chicago Corporation Mandinka, Merrill Lynch Masai Warriors and Northern Trust Ashanti.

While the players hail from the projects, the coaches and league administrators hail from the office towers of the Loop—guys like Bob Muzikowski, president of Benefit Planning Inc.; Jonathan Strain, vice president of Fifield Realty Corp.; and Doug Regan, an officer with the Northern Trust Company.

"I asked Al if the kids would use us as role models or if they would be turned off because basically we are just a bunch of yuppies," says Bill Vranos, an orthopedic surgeon resident who's coaching one of the teams. "I mean, there are guys coming up to the field in their suits and changing for practice right there. He said he didn't think it mattered; they are young enough that they don't know any better."

"For a bunch of white guys to [start] a league in Cabrini might not work," says Strain, a white guy who is the league's secretary. "We are trying to provide an infrastructure of finance and administration behind what already existed."

Despite this, doubt still emanates from the league's president, who happens to be Carter.

"My answer to them is, 'You manage your blue-chip company downtown,'" says Carter. "These are impoverished people you are dealing with. It might be good to take your picture with a little black boy and run back down—

See Cabrini, pg. 4

Bernie Lincicome
In the wake of the news

Fine, now we can start the playoffs

Chicago Tribune
NEW YORK—Next.

The playoffs may begin now.

Whatever that was against the Knickerbockers of New York, shadow boxing, calisthenics, dress rehearsal (the Knicks in the dresses), it was not playoff basketball's proudest moment.

It had nothing to do with what comes now and beyond for the Bulls.

"We know what's over the hill," said Michael Jordan.

That would be Philadelphia, astonishingly Philadelphia, a team that swept its betters in the Milwaukee Bucks, a team of considerable menace and due in Chicago on Saturday.

"They beat us twice in our place this year," said Jordan. "We took them in five in last year's playoffs. They'll remember that."

"Philadelphia," said Bulls coach Phil Jackson "is nothing to sneeze at."

These warnings sound less empty than those the Bulls coughed up to describe the Knicks, a duty but never a conviction.

The Knicks were grunt work for the Bulls, necessary and thankless, offering no hint of the chore ahead.

Except for the exercise, the Bulls might as well have faced this series in. Hardly worth the effort it took to avoid the human land mines that litter the happy avenues of the big city. One night in Manhattan is too many to confirm the obvious.

"They won 62 [actually 61] games, we won 39," said Knicks coach John MacLeod. "They were first, and we were eighth."

So, blame the NBA for this, for the waste of our time and their energy. The Knicks had no business littering the calendar.

"We were determined," conceded Jackson, "not to let anything unnatural happen."

Unnatural like losing, like hinting at losing, like giving the Knicks any reason to straighten the furniture in their very untidy house.

"We were a team on mission," Jackson said, "against a team a little thin chemistrywise."

Thank goodness they had no chemistry. The Knicks may have blown up themselves and the rare Bull they got close enough to recognize.

Jordan, maybe because it was Madison Square Garden, indulged in a bit of his signature filigree, as unnecessary here as it was in the Stadium, scoring 33 just to show it could be done when needed. The cheers were louder for Jordan than for the trophied Knick of the Year, Patrick Ewing.

(Being Knick of the Year is, I assume, still an honor.)

Ewing was exposed as a rather large mutt who surrenders easily.

"We need to focus on the future now," Ewing said, "and try to turn things around."

The future, for Ewing, seldom lasts past

See Lincicome, pg. 2

INSIDE

Countdown to the Derby

■ After some rough times, trainer David Cross is back at Churchill Downs. Page 3.
■ Bluegrass Country is the world's racehorse capital. But why? Back Page.

NBA

Bulls 103, Knicks 94	Lakers 94, Rockets 90
Pistons 103, Hawks 91	Sonics 107, Blazers 99
76ers 121, Bucks 100	Jazz 107, Suns 96

Roundup, Page 3

AL	NL
Brewers 8, Sox 2	Cubs 10, Astros 3
Mariners 6, Orioles 3	Reds 4, Pirates 3
Red Sox 7, Twins 5	Expos 1, Dodgers 0
Tigers 13, Royals 7	Cardinals 5, Braves 3
Rangers 8, Blue Jays 5	Phillies 11, Giants 9
A's 7, Yankees 3	Mets 6, Padres 3
Angels 6, Indians 5	Roundups, Page 5

How sweep it is! Bulls beat Knicks

By Sam Smith
Chicago Tribune

NEW YORK—The exclamation point is perhaps the most favored punctuation mark in this city, where the cries "Help!" "Look out!" and "Stop, thief!" are often heard.

Tuesday in Madison Square Garden, those words were on the lips of the New York Knicks as the Bulls slammed their playoff dreams to the ground and stole their hopes in a 103-94 victory. It gave the Bulls a three-game sweep in the opening-round series.

The Bulls now open the Eastern Conference semifinals Saturday in the Stadium against the Philadelphia 76ers.

"This ballclub was determined to go through the Knicks and not let anything unnatural happen, like an upset," said Bulls coach Phil Jackson. "It was a great game by Michael Jordan [33 points, six steals] and Scottie Pippen [21 points, 11 rebounds, four steals] and great relief help from Will Perdue [a career-high 16 points and 10 rebounds], and there were a number of people who contributed along the way."

But not like Jordan and Pippen, who placed their own unique exclamation points on the game in the second quarter after the Knicks had taken a 12-point lead.

"It was an exclamation mark done with a fury," said Jackson.

Bulls-76er tickets on sale at 10 a.m.

Playoff tickets for the Bulls-Philadelphia series will go on sale at 10 a.m. Wednesday at the Stadium, all Ticketron outlets or by calling 312-902-1919.

The series opens with a noon game Saturday at the Stadium. Dates and times of future games have not yet been determined.

■ Philadelphia and Los Angeles complete first-round playoff sweeps. Page 3.

"I was concerned at that time and it was a good comeback to gain control of the game in a short period of time."

First, Pippen blew down the lane and rose up, up and slammed over Patrick Ewing.

"It was a point to make that we were going to take the ball to the hole," Pippen said.

Eleven of the Bulls' 12 second-quarter baskets—and 27 of 43 for the game—were layups or slams.

"We were going to attack the basket and we weren't going to change our game plan," Pippen said.

That brought the Bulls within
See Bulls, pg. 2

Scottie Pippen slams over the Knicks' Patrick Ewing during the Bulls' 103-94 victory Tuesday night in New York. Pippen scored 21 points as the Bulls won the best-of-five playoff series 3-0.
AP Laserphoto

For Pacers, he can be key person

By Skip Myslenski
Chicago Tribune

INDIANAPOLIS—Chuck Person, Indiana's mercurial forward, is being good. Really. He is just sitting placidly in an empty Market Square Arena, his hands demurely folded, and when he speaks, his tones are as mellifluous as those of a mother cooing to her 2-year-old daughter. Good, that is what Chuck Person is being here.

He is exhibiting none of that combativeness he showed last Friday in Boston Garden, where he was both physical and mouthy with Larry Bird during the Celtics' Game 1 victory over the Pacers. Nor are his emotions as roiling as they were last Sunday in Boston Garden, where he helped even their series with a playoff-record seven "threes" on his way to scoring 39 points.

"Reggie, let me have one more three. Reggie, I want one more three," he yelled late in that game as teammate Reggie Miller dribbled time off the clock.

"I love it," he then chortled after that clock had reached zero. "National TV. Parquet floor. Those [expletive] banners. The leprechauns. They were all trying to stop me, and no one did."

No. There is none of that here some 30 hours before the Celts and Pacers meet in Wednesday's
See Pacers, pg. 2

Astros first baseman Jeff Bagwell tags out Gary Scott on a rundown in Tuesday night's game. Scott hit his first major-league home run in the Cubs' 10-3 victory.
Tribune photo by Jim Prisching

Villanueva powers Cub rout

By Bill Jauss

"When I'm hitting the ball," said Hector Villanueva, with a big smile, "people say I'm strong. When I'm not hitting, they say I'm fat."

He spoke as a strong man Tuesday night. Following George Bell's reminder to stay back on the pitch, Villanueva hit a 2-2 fastball for a three-run third-inning home run as the Cubs beat the Houston Astros 10-3 in Wrigley Field.

The 240-pound catcher was inserted into the starting lineup because Damon Berryhill is hitting .130 and Joe Girardi is injured. Villanueva also doubled off the left-field wall. He singled home another run. His four RBIs was his major-league high.

But first and foremost, Villanueva thinks of himself as a catcher. So when he first saw that a west wind was whipping at 22 m.p.h. from home plate toward the outfield walls, his first concern was not his own swings but those of the Astros.

"I thought of my pitcher, Mike Bielecki, and how he had to keep the ball down so they wouldn't hit too many out of him," said Villanueva.

While Bielecki did not have
See Cubs, pg. 2

Fernandez fails again as Sox fall

By Alan Solomon
Chicago Tribune

MILWAUKEE—What's wrong with Alex Fernandez? Probably nothing. Maybe something. But his last three starts have been brutal.

Tuesday night, Fernandez was hit early and often as the White Sox dropped an 8-2 non-thriller to the Milwaukee Brewers in chilly, blustery County Stadium.

The 9,136 on hand—the smart ones under blankets, the smartest sleeping through part or all of the snappy 3 hours 39 minutes—saw a pitcher going through something he's never gone through before.

"I don't know if he's had much failure out there on the mound," said manager Jeff Torborg.

Fernandez (2-2) has had a dose of it in his last three starts. The six runs he gave up Tuesday night marked the third time in those three starts he has given up six—which is nice symmetry but has pushed his earned-run average up to 8.55. The first start in that sequence lasted one inning.

In his last 12 innings, he has had 33 baserunners. Tuesday night, there were nine hits, four walks and a hit batsman in four-
See Sox, pg. 4

JORDAN TIME SPELLS BEDTIME FOR SIXERS

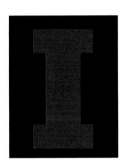

In the second-round playoff series versus Philadelphia, much like during the regular season, the Bulls avoided "Jordan Time" like some disease.

In this, the season of equal opportunity, sharing the bill on offense was the word.

Still, watching Jordan take over during the Game 5 win May 14 was nothing short of spectacular and put the Sixers to sleep for the season.

Jordan scored the final 12 Bulls' points in the 100-95 clincher, finishing with a game-high 38 points and 19 rebounds.

"He just took over when he had to," said 76ers guard Rickey Green.

Indeed, Jordan, after suffering through a poor shooting first half, exploded in the third quarter for 13 points.

Then, when Charles Barkley led a charge that knotted the score at 92 with 3:10 to play, Jordan took his game another level higher.

"I thought we had a good shot," said 76ers coach Jim Lynam. "But Jordan took over."

The Bulls executed all series long, easily handling the Sixers in the opener at the Stadium, 105-92.

Despite game-highs of 34 points and 11 rebounds from Charles Barkley, the Bulls coasted with defense.

"Our defense has been our offense in the last four [playoff] games, and it's been a team defense, not a one-individual defense," said Michael Jordan who led the Bulls in Game 1 with a quiet 29 points.

Jordan again tallied 29 points to spark the 112-100 Game 2 win May 6, but the Bulls turned in a team

By Sam Smith

performance, this time dominating on the boards.

"[Bill] Cartwright and [Will] Perdue are definitely hurting us [a combined eight offensive rebounds and 21 points], and we need to keep them off the offensive boards," said Barkley.

The only blemish during the series came in Game 3, when the action moved to Philadelphia. Hersey Hawkins, who led the 76ers with 29 points, drilled a three-point basket with 10.3 seconds remaining to hand the Bulls their first loss of the playoffs.

Jordan's 46 points couldn't save the 99-97 decision, a win that led Philadelphia coach Jim Lynam to believe, "the emotion is with us now."

The Bulls quickly squelched any ideas of a momentum swing by taking Game 4 in Philadelphia 101-85.

The Mother's Day win was a testament to the equal opportunity Bulls offense, with Jordan (25), Horace Grant (22) and Pippen (20) all hitting double figures.

"Everybody was playing well and making good contributions, and I wasn't overworking," said Jordan. "Who could you point to to try to stop? You stop Pippen, you're going to get hurt by Grant and Cartwright and [John] Paxson and Jordan."

But more significant was how the Bulls hurt the 76ers, in their pride and in their play. Losing a home game and scoring just 85 points—Philadelphia's lowest total in nine years—took enough wind out of their sails for the Bulls to blow them away in the clincher. ■

Michael Jordan, here scoring over Hersey Hawkins, led a team effort in the 4-1 win.
PHOTO BY JIM PRISCHING

WILL CALL FOR PERDUE

C heers, not jeers, cascaded down on Will Perdue when he left the action during the series-clinching win over Philadelphia. Perdue was probably too preoccupied to notice the majority of the fans were standing—it was only the second quarter of a taut game—but, indeed, the fans serenaded their once-designated boobird with the ultimate tribute. He had entered Game 5 with the Bulls clinging to a one-point lead. When he exited, some seven minutes later, the Bulls were leading by six. During that stretch, Perdue slammed over 7-foot-7-inch Manute Bol, drilled a pair of 15-footers, scored on a layup and grabbed three rebounds. "I've had better games," he said. "But as far as appreciation goes, that was the best I've had. The fans are starting to appreciate the hard work."

Composite box: Bulls vs. 76ers

BULLS (4-1)	G	Avg min	FG pct	FT pct	Reb	Ast	Avg pts
Jordan	5	39.2	.489	.795	40	39	33.4
Pippen	5	42.2	.573	.867	47	30	23.4
Grant	5	40.0	.540	.714	46	14	12.8
Cartwright	5	29.6	.536	.636	27	13	10.2
Armstrong	5	18.4	.461	.600	8	11	5.4
Hodges	5	13.4	.348	–	0	6	4.2
Paxson	5	27.4	.579	1.000	24	13	5.0
Perdue	5	13.8	.591	.250	22	2	5.4
King	5	8.6	.333	.500	7	1	1.4
Hopson	5	1.2	.500	.600	2	0	1.0
Williams	5	1.4	.250	–	2	0	0.4
Levingston	5	4.8	.333	–	5	0	0.4
Totals	**5**	**–**	**.511**	**.728**	**210**	**130**	**103**

Three-point goals: 10-31, .323 (Hodges 5-11, Jordan 2-11, Pippen 2-5, Paxson 1-3, Armstrong 0-1). **Team rebounds:** 37. **Blocked shots:** 15. **Turnovers:** 49. **Steals:** 38. **Technical fouls:** 3. **Flagrant foul:** None. **Illegal defenses:** 1.

76ERS (1-4)	G	Avg min	FG pct	FT pct	Reb	Ast	Avg pts
Barkley	5	41.0	.640	.646	51	27	25.6
Gilliam	5	35.4	.428	.871	31	7	16.2
Mahorn	5	23.4	.333	.500	19	4	2.6
Green	5	23.0	.389	1.000	5	13	6.6
Hawkins	5	40.4	.431	.953	29	15	19.8
Bol	5	14.6	.461	.625	12	1	3.5
Anderson	5	28.4	.320	.833	11	14	7.6
Turner	5	25.0	.371	.833	9	21	7.6
Reid	5	5.4	.375	–	5	1	1.2
Williams	5	1.4	.750	–	4	0	1.2
Oliver	5	1.0	.667	1.000	0	1	1.2
Hoppen	5	1.0	1.000	–	2	0	1.2
Totals	**5**	**–**	**.453**	**.806**	**178**	**104**	**94.2**

Three-point goals: 14-39, .359 (Hawkins 8-14, Barkley 1-10, Turner 2-7, Anderson 1-4, Green 2-3, Reid 0-1). **Team rebounds:** 39. **Blocked shots:** 20. **Turnovers:** 61. **Steals:** 33. **Technical fouls:** 4. **Flagrant foul:** 2. **Illegal defense:** 3.

Chicago Tribune

Sports

Section 4 ★ Wednesday, May 15, 1991

Need for racing success still driving Haas

By Robert Markus
Chicago Tribune

INDIANAPOLIS—Carl Haas kicked off his loafers and sprawled on the couch at the rear of the Newman-Haas motor home, the picture of relaxation.

It was a totally atypical pose for the self-confessed workaholic who quietly has built an auto racing empire on Chicago's North Shore.

On one arm of the sofa was a white plastic ashtray with an unlit but well-chewed cigar that appeared to be about six inches shorter than one of Andre Dawson's bats.

Clenched in Haas' teeth was another pristine cigar, which has become the trademark of the 61-year-old Chicago-born entrepreneur.

Actor Paul Newman, who is the Newman half of Newman-Haas Racing, likes to say of his partner that "the core of his mind rests in his cigar—and it's a good cigar."

It's a first-rate cigar, as is everything Carl Haas owns.

"It's my big vice," Haas says, "although I do more chewing than smoking now. When they get too soggy, I pitch 'em. When you're spending 50 grand a mile on a race car, a couple of cigars aren't going to change it a lot."

The cost of racing—as well as the cost of a good smoke—has gone up considerably since the days when he was driving himself in the 1950s.

"I didn't have any money," he recalls, "but things were a lot cheaper in those days. My first MG cost about $1,700, and I traded it in for a Porsche Speedster that was, I think, about $3,300."

The sophisticated Lola race cars with which Haas now campaigns in the Indianapolis 500 and the rest of the PPG-CART series cost upwards of $500,000 each. Driving the costly machines for the Newman-Haas team in this year's Indy are Mario and Michael Andretti, the famed father-son duo who are positioned third (first row) and fifth (second row) in the race lineup after the first weekend of qualifying.

He maintains the cars in a 32,000-square foot facility in Lincolnshire that also houses his primary businesses. Haas is the North American importer of Lola and Reynard race cars and Hewland

See Haas, pg. 8

Tribune photo by Frank Hanes

Carl Haas and his trademark unlit cigar.

Bernie Lincicome
In the wake of the news

Sixers can't find case against Bulls

Like taking candy from a bully.

There wasn't much to Philadelphia after all; little but bulk and bluster and, in both cases, Charles Barkley.

Not enough, not nearly enough, to extend the Bulls anywhere near to nervousness, never mind defeat.

"A good playoff for us," Phil Jackson would say.

Four out of five isn't perfect, but four out of five is good enough for possibly a week off now, good enough as a preview of coming distractions, a third conference final series in the last three years.

There was little in either series against the Knicks and the 76ers to show that the Bulls cannot get to where they want to go.

"I think these playoffs have shown the variety of skills this team has," said Jackson. "Scottie Pippen. The versatility of Horace Grant. Bill Cartwright doing the job inside."

"We've shown that we are a good board team, no matter our size. And our defense has just been tremendous. Only one game did they get 100."

Detroit or Boston awaits, though the winner might have to be carted into the Stadium on a litter.

The Bulls were playing for a purpose. The 76ers were playing for pride. It was no contest.

In the end, when it mattered, there was Michael Jordan, dancing off towards more of the same, on to another game, scoring all the points the Bulls would need and all in a row.

From 92-92 and three minutes to play, Jordan scored the last eight for the Bulls, while the 76ers could manage only a three-point basket from Hersey Hawkins.

Sixer coach Jim Lynam was asked if he had ever seen anybody who could take over a game like Jordan.

"Probably not," he said softly. "With all the things he can do, probably not."

And there was the grand Barkley, all early grunts and late misses—just four fourth-quarter points—throwing up the last shot of Philadelphia's season, a clunker from somewhere beyond hope, for it would have taken a five-pointer to tie.

The ball, indifferent to dreams, bounced once, high and to the right, into Jordan's hands.

Sweet irony, sweet ending.

The two men would hug with honest affection one for the other.

"Charles fought like a warrior," Jordan would say.

Barkley would next consider what he must do to get where Jordan is going, and Jordan

See Lincicome, pg. 2

Jordan finishes off Sixers

Tribune photo by Jim Prisching

Michael Jordan scoops in two points over Philadelphia's Hersey Hawkins in Tuesday night's game. Jordan had 38 points and 19 rebounds in the Bulls' 100-95 victory.

Takes over in stretch to save Bulls' victory

By Sam Smith

If the British, two centuries ago, had been as impressive as the Bulls in marching through New York and Philadelphia, everyone now would be drinking warm beer and celebrating royalty.

And, in fact, that's just about what they were doing in the Stadium Tuesday night as the Bulls, led by his highness Michael Jordan with 38 points and 19 rebounds, wrapped up the Eastern Conference semifinals with a 100-95 victory over the Philadelphia 76ers.

They took this series four games to one after sweeping the New York Knicks in the opening playoff round.

The Bulls' 13th straight home playoff victory made them 7-1 overall in this season's playoffs, and they moved into the conference finals for the third straight season. They'll take on the winner of the Boston-Detroit series.

"It makes no difference to me who we play," said Bulls coach Phil Jackson.

The Bulls will not find out who'll they'll meet at least until Friday, and possibly not until Sunday if the Celtics-Pistons series goes seven games. In that case, the Bulls would not begin play in the conference finals until early next week, probably Tuesday. Otherwise, they'd start Sunday in the Stadium.

But Tuesday, they came awfully close to looking at a return trip to Philadelphia when the 76ers, led by Charles Barkley's 30 points, fought back from 10 points down after three quarters to tie the score at 92 with 3:10 left.

"I thought we had a good shot," said 76ers coach Jim Lynam. "But Jordan took over."

After shooting 6 of 16 for 13 points in the first half while Scottie Pippen carried the Bulls with 24 points, Jordan scored 13

See Bulls, pg. 2

Tribune photo by Jim Prisching

Horace Grant leads the celebration as the final horn confirms the Bulls series-clinching victory over the 76ers Tuesday night.

76ers' best effort still comes up short

The 76ers' gave it their best shot Tuesday, but it just wasn't good enough to knock off the Bulls. Page 2.

Blazers, Lakers make Western finals

Portland eliminates Utah, and the Los Angeles Lakers oust Golden State in the Western Conference semifinals. Page 2.

INSIDE

Bolton stops White Sox cold

Unbeaten Tom Bolton gets his fourth victory and Ellis Burks homers as Boston beats the White Sox 4-1. Page 3.

Parcells reportedly quitting

Bill Parcells, head coach of the Super Bowl champion New York Giants, is reportedly ready to step down. Page 3.

Lockport gains revenge

No. 1 Lockport posts a 1-0 victory over defending state champ Thornwood. Page 4.

NBA

Bulls 100, 76ers 95	Blazers 103, Jazz 96
Lakers 124, Warriors 119	**Stories, Page 2**

AL	NL
Red Sox 4, White Sox 1	Cubs 5, Braves 4
Yankees 7, Angels 1	Reds 3, Cardinals 1
Mariners 2, Indians 1	Pirates 6, Astros 3
Blue Jays 4, Orioles 1	Mets 6, Padres 1
Twins 5, Brewers 1	Dodgers 6, Expos 2
Orioles 6, Athletics 1	Phillies 9, Giants 0
Rangers 5, Tigers 3	**Roundups, Page 5**

Espositos hoping to make Lightning strike

By Mike Kiley
Chicago Tribune

TAMPA—Some ideas don't automatically compute. Madonna blushing. Norman Schwarzkopf out of a job. George Steinbrenner suffering in silence. Hockey in Florida.

But at least one of those is going to happen. You can mark it on your calendar. October 1992, the Tampa Bay Lightning makes its National Hockey League debut. Air-conditioning in Florida will take on a new meaning.

The Stanley Cup opens Wednesday night in Pittsburgh, where the Minnesota North Stars hope to complete their Cinderella tale, but you already can hear a different beat in the South than ocean waves crashing. The sound of slap shots is building in some imaginations.

Phil and Tony Esposito, brothers famous for their NHL playing careers, hope to find their first front-office success in operating the Lightning. They are confident of getting the same kind of full house at the opener they encountered last Wednesday at the Hurricane Lounge in Port Richey, Fla., an hour north of Tampa.

An estimated 400 jammed the bowling alley-sports bar to see the Espositos, who now are moonlighting frequently after a day at the office by attending hockey nights in surrounding towns. These two never needed an excuse to have a beer, so Florida must seem like heaven to them.

Some fans at the Hurricane wore hats and T-shirts that represented a broad cross-section of NHL teams. There was a Rangers insignia, of course, because lounge boss Pete Graffanino hails from New York and told plenty of stories about Phil and Tony's playing days. But there was also outerwear advertising the Blackhawks, Boston Bruins, Hartford Whalers, Edmonton Oilers, St. Louis Blues,

See Espositos, pg. 7

Tribune photo by Bob Langer

Time for Keenan to make decision

Blackhawks management wants Mike Keenan to decide when he will relinquish his coaching duties to concentrate on being general manager. Page 3.

Dawson HR delivers Cubs' 'biggest win'

By Bill Jauss

"I let him provide the power," said Andre Dawson.

And with those six words, the Cubs' incomparable slugger said something that might prove as significant to Cub fans later this summer than any formula Dr. Albert Einstein ever uttered to scientists about mass or force or relativity.

Dawson was explaining the formula he used Tuesday night to drive his game-winning, eighth-inning pinch home run that beat the Atlanta Braves 5-4 in what manager Don Zimmer called, "without question our biggest win all year.

"If we had lost, we'd be three games below .500 and might never get back. Now, maybe we've started something."

Zimmer didn't start Dawson or any other member of his regular outfield, but after replacement outfielder Chico Walker's two-run homer in the seventh tied the game 4-4, Zimmer knew whom to call upon to pinch-hit for pitcher Paul Assenmacher with two out and nobody on base in the eighth.

Dawson ripped at a first pitch from reliever Kurt Mercker. While a crowd of 31,446 fans shrieked, Dawson smashed a drive into the center-field bleachers just to the right of the 400-foot sign on the wall.

This prompted the obligatory question: With two out and nobody on base, were you trying for a home run?

"I just tried to drive it," answered Dawson. "I just didn't want to get cheated. He's a power pitcher. I let him supply the power.

"A fastball. Out over the outer half of the plate. It wasn't a bad pitch. About the only place I could hit it was up the middle or to right-center."

So much for the technical explanation. Now, for the emotional impact of the blow that climaxed a rally from a 4-1 deficit

See Cubs, pg. 4

Jordan and Barkley: Opposites Attract

They're both known for their tongues.

Michael Jordan's is more famous, his tongue flashing as a sort of symbol of his daring flights to the basket for acrobatic, crowd-pleasing dunks.

Charles Barkley's is more infamous. His tongue has made him pro basketball's bad boy, the most penalized player in the NBA and perhaps the most controversial.

Michael Jordan is Wally Cleaver. Charles Barkley is Eddie Haskell. Jordan is Oliver Twist to Barkley's Artful Dodger. Michael Jordan spits in the face of convention with his gravity-defying game. Charles Barkley merely spits.

But when Jordan and Barkley embraced after Game 2 of the Eastern Conference semifinals May 6 at the Stadium, it was no made-for-TV show.

The two stars rate highly with one another.

"Maybe Rod Higgins and Barkley," Jordan says of the opposing players to whom he is closest. "You don't have the time to get close with too many guys."

"We're friends," Barkley says, "because most of the guys in this league are jerks and you wouldn't want to spend any time with them."

Of course, Jordan didn't put it quite that way, but he may have been thinking it.

"Charles is a freewheeling guy," Jordan says admiringly. "He says what's on his mind. It's like I'm the good brother and he's the bad brother. He says a lot of things the good brother wants to say but doesn't, and I like that."

Their talents make them among the top players in the league, but no two players in the NBA are perceived to be more different. Jordan is every mother's son. Barkley is just a son of a gun.

But they have come to enjoy each other's company.

When Jordan played in a charity golf tournament in Philadelphia last summer, Barkley served as his caddie. When Jordan started wearing a No. 23 earring last fall, Barkley admired it and Jordan got him a No. 34. They went overseas to do basketball clinics together last summer and play golf in a celebrity tournament.

"He's competitive at everything," says Jordan, the far superior golfer. "I've got to give him a shot and a half a hole, but he wants to bet on everything. He gets up there and takes this huge swing and the ball goes maybe 20 yards. But we have fun."

That's been the story for Jordan and Barkley since the 1984 Olympic Trials.

"We first met at the Pan Am Games the year before," Jordan recalls. "He was guarding me and knocked me out of bounds and into the stands when I tried to get by him. Then he just laughed."

They're both 28. Jordan was born Feb. 17, 1963, three days before Barkley. They were raised in the South, Barkley in Alabama, Jordan in North Carolina. They both sparkle in the spotlight, from the top of their shaven heads to the bottom of their games. And they're both about the same height, Jordan probably about an inch taller, though not the same size.

"You can tell he eats more," said Jordan.

The only difference is, Jordan goes under and over and around. Barkley goes through. But they get to the same place, even if Barkley sometimes arrives with his foot in his mouth.

In the end, the Bulls beat the Sixers in their playoff series. Philadelphia's season was over, but Jordan and Barkley remained friends. – Sam Smith

> '**C**harles is a freewheeling guy.'
> - Michael Jordan
>
> **The competition over, Barkley and Jordan remain friends.**
> **Photo by Jim Prisching**

The Pistons had unceremoniously eliminated the Bulls from the playoffs three seasons running. To change things, a team effort was needed. And Michael Jordan's quote after Game 1 was music to the ears of the Bulls' second-team players. "You have to give my supporting cast a lot of credit," he said. Indeed, the bench was instrumental in the 94-83 series-opening win at the Stadium. Will Perdue, Cliff Levingston, B.J. Armstrong and Craig Hodges were all on the court during a key, fourth-quarter surge that gave the Bulls a nine-point lead. "I think this showed we're more than a one-man team; [we're] not one individual," said Hodges.

Michael Jordan epitomized the Bulls' desire to outscrap Detroit in 1991. PHOTO BY BOB LANGER

Michael Jordan was his old self in Game 2, scoring 35 points in a 105-97 Bulls' win. But the real key was team defense. "They took us out of everything," said Pistons coach Chuck Daly.

John Paxson pressured Isiah Thomas and the Pistons into uncharacteristic panic.
PHOTO BY BOB LANGER

'**A**ll they did was complain the whole time. Why doesn't [Jordan] buy the team? He has all the money.'
    - Dennis Rodman

'**W**e wanted to let them know they're not going to intimidate us with the little cheap stuff.'
    - Michael Jordan

Jordan and Rodman went jaw-to-jaw.
PHOTO BY BOB LANGER

BULLS TAKE OUT TRASH

Bernie Lincicome

IN THE WAKE OF THE NEWS

Good riddance.

May the Pistons rest in pieces. In fact, it ought to be a requirement.

The NBA should consider Detroit so dangerous to the good health of basketball, not to mention to general decency, that they break it up and send its various parts to places so distant that it can never be reassembled.

Dennis Rodman, the smirking vermin, should be sent first and the farthest away, someplace without a ZIP code, running water or a decent mattress.

Bill Laimbeer, the sucker-punching oaf, needs a long rest in a tight suit, one of those with arms that tie in the back.

Isiah Thomas, the sneaky little puppeteer of this mob, ought never again be given anything sharp to play with, unless he turns it on himself.

The whole, thuggish bunch of them, including our nascent Olympic coach, Chuck Daly, should be frisked before being allowed to enter public places.

I hope I am not being unkind. Or too provincial about this.

This may not have been a good time to bring up the evil essence of Pistondom to Daly, since tears still puddled in his eyes after an emotional locker room farewell to his defeated menagerie.

Well, I suppose Ma Barker cried when she said goodbye to her boys too.

"I've seen the same thing from your club," Daly said.

While I am grateful that Daly thought enough to give me a share of the Bulls, I'm not certain that Jerry Reinsdorf would be necessarily thrilled to have me as a new partner.

"It isn't my team," I said.

"Aren't you from Chicago?" Daly asked.

Horace Grant helps slam the door on the Pistons' hopes for a three-peat.
Photo By Ed Wagner

Composite box: Bulls vs. Pistons

BULLS (4-0)	G	Avg min	FG pct	FT pct	Reb	Ast	Avg pts
Jordan	4	40.0	.535	.833	21	28	29.8
Pippen	4	38.8	.475	.769	31	21	22.0
Grant	4	37.8	.690	.700	31	8	13.5
Cartwright	4	30.8	.543	.500	21	5	10.5
Armstrong	4	19.8	.529	.800	10	15	7.0
Paxson	4	28.0	.400	1.000	5	15	6.5
Levingston	4	15.3	.455	.500	17	2	5.8
Hodges	4	12.0	.438	1.000	0	3	4.8
King	1	3.0	.400	–	2	0	4.0
Perdue	4	12.5	.455	.500	19	1	3.3
Williams	4	3.8	.667	.500	6	0	2.5
Hopson	1	3.0	.000	.500	1	0	1.0
Totals	**4**	–	**.515**	**.738**	**164**	**98**	**106.8**

Three-point goals: 7-23, .304 (Jordan 3-5, Armstrong 2-2, Hodges 2-6, Paxson 0-5, Pippen 0-4, Williams 0-1). **Team rebounds:** 52. **Blocked shots:** 27. **Turnovers:** 51. **Steals:** 37. **Technical fouls:** 3. **Illegal defenses:** 3. **Flagrant fouls:** 1.

PISTONS (0-4)	G	Avg min	FG pct	FT pct	Reb	Ast	Avg pts
Johnson	4	29.0	.587	.769	22	12	21.0
Aguirre	4	31.5	.453	.824	11	5	16.8
Thomas	4	37.8	.407	.724	19	24	16.5
Dumars	4	39.5	.347	.813	8	10	12.5
Laimbeer	4	22.0	.500	1.000	22	3	6.8
Salley	4	17.0	.533	.733	10	2	6.8
Edwards	4	18.8	.400	.833	5	2	6.3
Rodman	4	29.5	.444	–	30	2	4.5
Hastings	2	5.0	.667	–	3	0	2.5
Bedford	2	8.0	.000	1.000	7	2	2.0
Rollins	3	9.0	1.000	–	2	0	1.3
Henderson	3	2.3	.400	–	0	3	1.3
Totals	**4**	–	**.456**	**.786**	**139**	**65**	**95.3**

Three-point goals: 12-39, .308 (Aguirre 5-9, Rodman 2-7, Dumars 3-10, Thomas 1-4, Laimbeer 0-2, Johnson 0-1, Henderson 0-1, Hastings 1-2, Bedford 0-2). **Team rebounds:** 33. **Blocked shots:** 13. **Turnovers:** 60 . **Steals:** 32. **Technical fouls:** 7. **Flagrant fouls:** 4. **Illegal defenses:** 1.

"Yes," I admitted with what I hoped was the same degree of pride as I would have in any of the last three years. Having a pro basketball team in the NBA finals does not make Chicago any better today than it was yesterday, though, gratefully, it also does not make it Detroit.

"The hardest fouls I've seen in the playoffs were by [Larry] Bird and [Michael] Jordan," Daly said.

What Rodman did to Scottie Pippen—shove him face-first into the floor—was equal to any blow ever struck in basketball or in Daly's imagination.

"We aren't champions yet," said Jordan.

Only very classy trash-removers. ∎

The Bulls, near the end of the
sweep of Detroit, enjoy their fourth
laughable win.
PHOTO BY JIM PRISCHING

FINAL

Michael and Magic. Hype and hope. As the league's two brightest stars meet for the first time in the trophy round, the city of Chicago looks past

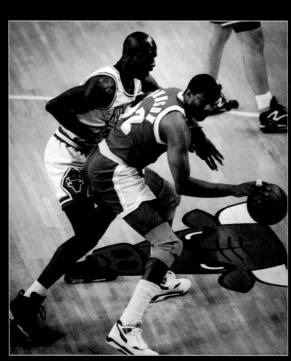

PHOTO BY NANCY STONE

the glitter and yearns for the glory of a first-ever NBA title. Soon, the wait would end and the party would begin.

S

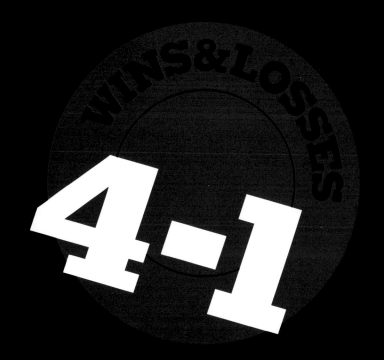

WINS&LOSSES

4-1

JACKSON BALANCES BULLS' ACT

In many ways, the Bulls, as they prepared to open the 1991 NBA Finals against the Lakers in the Stadium, had become Phil Jackson.

And not the Phil Jackson of the press clippings, the intellectual, New York Times crossword puzzle solver, Grateful Dead music fan, the man who distributes literature to players on the road, splices scenes from movies to dramatize his points, the onetime hippie, anti-establishment meditating left-hander with the ugly gait—and ties to match.

Sure, all of that is Phil Jackson. But it's the inner calm of Jackson under duress and pressure that rubbed off on this Bulls team. Sort of a grace under pressure, if you will. No thumps or bumps from Charles Barkley and Rick Mahorn were going to make a difference, no flagrant behavior by a worm and other critters were going to make them shake and shudder.

"The thing we really didn't have a grasp of before Phil," says John Paxson, "was how to respond to Detroit's aggressive nature."

"I think moderation of lifestyle is the key to this game," said Jackson, who learned most of his lessons under longtime Knicks coach Red Holzman.

"I think that's something you saw with Detroit. Talk about riding highs and then suffering lows because you ride too high. You saw how boisterous they acted when they won, and then they were as negative in their losses.

"I felt I could bring a sense of poise and I could help give this team self-determination."

Jackson took on a no-win job when he was named head coach after the 1988-89 season. He had been an assistant under Doug Collins. He was a solid role player for the Knicks teams of the early 1970s, and then a successful Continental Basketball Association coach. But he had never made a name for himself as a coach.

Now he was taking over a team that had just overachieved its way to the Eastern Conference finals.

And with expectations high, the Bulls simply had to do what only two teams do: Go to the NBA Finals.

By Sam Smith

And he'd talk to the team, telling them against Detroit that the water always wins against the rock, that the rock will stop the water for a while, but the water would move off in another direction and eventually wear down the rock.

The message: The Pistons pressure you here, slide there. Power doesn't win. Be pliable, he'd say, not rigid.

"Basketball is a game in which you can make mistakes, but if you make a mistake you can't let it smother you so you don't do well in the next sequence," he said. "There has to be a certain understanding of how to play and carry yourself as a basketball player.

"That demeanor is very important if you expect to win a championship."

Which for this year's Bulls, thanks to Phil Jackson, was just going about business as usual. ∎

Phil Jackson exhorts the Bulls during Game 1 of the NBA Finals against L.A. PHOTO BY NANCY STONE

As ADVERTISED

Bernie Lincicome

IN THE WAKE OF THE NEWS

So, that's how it's going to be. Exactly as advertised.

Let's hurry and cut right to Game 7 of this Bulls and Lakers adventure, because there may not be enough fingernails, antacid or VCR tape to get us there otherwise.

Give Michael Jordan his 30 a game and Magic Johnson his triple doubles, and we can use our breath for something less important than gasping at the pair of them, like breathing.

"This is the way basketball is supposed to be played," says Johnson.

This is the winner speaking, but it could have been the loser. In fact, it was.

"That was a great game," agrees Bulls coach Phil Jackson.

If this series continues as it has started, with a 93-91 Laker win, it will severely damage one of the most dependable of life's lessons: the greater the anticipation, the more certain the regret.

Coffee always smells better than it tastes. Blind dates need flea collars. American cars are going to expire the day before the warranty does.

You know what you know. And what you know is that no way was it possible for any basketball game to live up to the jangling hype that preceded this one.

All that this series is supposed to be was crystallized in the third quarter when the public address blurted out, "Assist to Magic Jordan."

If you are told before time that the game will have 22 lead changes, that neither side will get a double-digit advantage, that the pass for the winning basket will be made by Johnson, the passer, and the shot that doesn't drop will be a wide-open jumper by Jordan, the shooter, you nod and say that this isn't wrestling or roller derby.

It will not come down to legends doing what legends do, and one of them needing to do it better.

Irony is left for Sam Perkins. "It took a North Carolina guy to beat me," Jordan says.

It took a guy who is not supposed to be standing beyond the three-point line, throwing up a shot as if he is tossing a newspaper onto the roof.

"I had to get a little extra arch," Perkins explains.

With four seconds remaining, it was as crucial for Jordan to shoot the shot that lost the game as it would have been to win it.

"It rattled in and out," says Jordan.

"[We] got the nervousness out, so we will be ready for the game on Wednesday," says Jackson.

Can't wait. ∎

Michael Jordan is disgusted with the turn of events in Game 1 of the NBA Finals. PHOTO BY CHARLES CHERNEY

Game 1: Lakers 93, Bulls 91

LAKERS (93)	Min	FG-att	FT-att	Reb	Ast	Fls	Pts
Sam Perkins	30	8-17	3-6	4	0	1	22
James Worthy	45	11-24	0-0	3	1	2	22
Vlade Divac	44	5-11	6-6	14	1	4	16
Byron Scott	37	1-4	7-8	2	2	4	9
Magic Johnson	43	4-5	9-10	10	11	2	19
A.C. Green	16	0-1	3-4	3	0	0	3
Terry Teagle	10	1-3	0-0	1	0	1	2
Larry Drew	5	0-1	0-0	0	0	2	0
Totals	**240**	**30-66**	**28-34**	**37**	**15**	**16**	**93**

Percentages: FG .455, FT .824. **Three-point goals:** 5-10, .500 (Johnson 2-2, Perkins 3-4, Worthy 0-2, Scott 0-1, Drew 0-1). **Team rebounds:** 6. **Blocked shots:** 3 (Divac 3). **Turnovers:** 13 (Johnson 5, Divac 4, Worthy 2, Perkins, Teagle). **Steals:** 7 (Divac 3, Perkins, Worthy, Scott, Johnson). **Technical fouls:** None. **Illegal defense:** None.

BULLS (91)	Min	FG-att	FT-att	Reb	Ast	Fls	Pts
Scottie Pippen	41	7-19	5-7	7	5	5	19
Horace Grant	40	3-8	0-0	10	1	1	6
Bill Cartwright	34	3-8	0-0	4	2	4	6
John Paxson	30	3-7	0-0	4	2	2	6
Michael Jordan	40	14-24	7-9	8	12	5	36
Craig Hodges	13	2-5	0-0	0	0	0	4
Cliff Levingston	20	1-2	0-0	2	1	0	2
Will Perdue	12	2-2	2-2	4	0	2	6
B.J. Armstrong	10	3-5	0-0	0	3	2	6
Totals	**240**	**38-80**	**14-18**	**39**	**26**	**21**	**91**

Percentage: FG .475, FT .778. **Three-point goals:** 1-7, .143 (Jordan 1-1, Paxson 0-1, Armstrong 0-1, Pippen 0-2, Hodges 0-2). **Team rebounds:** 6. **Blocked shots:** 5 (Pippen 2, Cartwright, Levingston, Perdue). **Turnovers:** 10 (Jordan 4, Pippen 3, Grant, Hodges, Levingston). **Steals:** 11 (Jordan 3, Grant 2, Levingston 2, Pippen, Armstrong). **Technical fouls:** None. **Illegal defense:** None.

L.A. Lakers	29	22	24	18	—93
CHICAGO BULLS	30	23	15	23	—91

A: 18,676. T: 2:29. Officials: H. Evans, H. Hollins, J. Madden.

OVERWHELMING IN OVERTIME

hen the Lakers' last, desperate, hopeless shot finally floated down to Michael Jordan, he cradled the ball in one hand and with his other hammered the floor in defiant triumph. Like hammering another nail into the

Lakers' coffin? Could be that's what the Bulls did with their thrilling 104-96 overtime victory in Game 3 of the NBA Finals.

As the Bulls prepared for Game 4 here June 9, they knew they had wrestled back the home-court advantage they lost in Game 1 and perhaps taken the Lakers' best shot along with a 2-1 series lead.

"We can never underestimate this team," said Michael Jordan, who scored 29 points, including a 14-foot jumper with 3.4 seconds left that sent the game into overtime and six points in the extra period. "But we did take a good shot. They extended the lead in the third quarter [going ahead by 13], but we were able to fight back and win.

"It will be tough for them to swallow, mentally, because they have to feel they gave one away."

This was to be a Lakers coronation before an adoring throng in the Forum. Magic Johnson was electric in scoring 22 points and handing off for 10 more baskets. Sam Perkins had 25 points, and Vlade Divac was elusive in scoring 24 before fouling out in overtime.

But the Bulls left the Lakers walking out with a sag in their shoulders and an emptiness in their eyes.

"We just didn't hit our shots," said Johnson. "And their offensive rebounds killed us."

That was a tribute to Horace Grant, who had a career-equaling playoff high 22 points and 11 rebounds, and Scottie Pippen, who had 19 points and

By Sam Smith

tied a career playoff high with 13 rebounds before fouling out late in regulation.

"I had talked to Horace going into the last game," said Pippen, "and we made a conscious effort to keep moving, to screen each other's man so we could get to the boards and get the second shots."

And it was big, the Bulls outrebounding L.A. 46-29, including a 16-9 advantage in offensive boards. The Lakers' 29 rebounds were an all-time low for the Finals.

But in the end it would come down to Jordan, who suffered a mild sprain of his right big toe on the last shot of regulation.

"It's sore," said Jordan, who will play Sunday. "I landed wrong. But I made the shot."

And it enabled the Bulls to send the game into overtime after a thrilling game that sent fans traveling from peaks of hope to valleys of despair.

The Bulls had come charging back against overwhelming odds after the Lakers' 18-2 run in the third quarter had given them a 67-54 lead.

After that, Cliff Levingston came through with his finest performance of the year, picking up a steal, a block, two key rebounds and a tip-in on the way to 10 points to give the Bulls' bench an 18-6 scoring margin over the Laker reserves.

"I was just trying to do some things to help change momentum," said Levingston. "L.A. was starting to make another surge, and we needed something."

Levingston capped his burst with a tip-in to give the

LIGHTS OUT FOR THE LAKERS

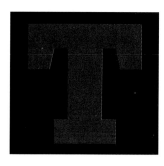

They sparkled like the sun glinting off Lake Michigan and were as sweet as icing on a birthday cake. In a glorious party at the Stadium, the Bulls evened the NBA Finals at 1-1 June 5 by blowing out the Lakers 107-86 with a brilliant all-around team performance.

"Everyone contributed," said Michael Jordan, who contributed the most with 33 points and 13 assists, hitting a remarkable 15 of 18 shots, 10 of 11 in the second half.

"I was surprised we won by the margin we did. But we reverted to what we had been doing in the 12 [playoff] games before Game 1. We picked up our defensive intensity and got everyone involved."

By Sam Smith

The Bulls set an all-time shooting record for the Finals at 61.7 percent while holding the Lakers to 41.1 percent, their low in these playoffs.

Horace Grant, overshadowed by Sam Perkins in Game 1, slipped inside for 20 points on 10 for 13 shooting while Perkins settled for a meaningless 11. "Horace was a force inside," said Magic Johnson.

John Paxson, often overlooked in Game 1, took advantage of every look he got at the basket, knocking in all eight of his shots for 16 points. He combined with Jordan for a 10 for 10 third quarter when the Bulls took control by outscoring the Lakers 38-26. In the quarter, the Bulls hit an unbelievable 17 of 20 shots.

"I told John," said Jordan, who played a lot at point guard, "that if we were going to go down, there shouldn't be any bullets in his holster. He had to keep shooting."

The Bulls also got a big-time shot in the arm from Pippen on defense as he pressured Johnson upcourt, making it harder for the Lakers to get into their offense. Magic was held to 14 points on 4 for 13 shooting and 10 assists.

Pippen scored 20 points and added 10 assists in an invaluable all-around effort. "I just tried to defend full-court and make him [Johnson] work hard and try to wear him down," said Pippen.

Things became clearer for the Bulls in a lot of ways. Grant reverted to his prescription goggles on the court for the first time since the opening round of the playoffs, and the basket began to come into focus for him with 10 first-quarter points.

Meanwhile, the Bulls began to focus on the defense that has carried them to the Finals for the first time in franchise history.

"Our energy was defensive," said coach Phil Jackson.

"Everyone admitted how nervous they were in the first game," said Jordan, "but tonight we came out to play."

"It's a game you rarely see at this time of the season," said James Worthy, who led the Lakers with 24. "It's not embarrassing, just disappointing. But it's part of a seven-game series. It's not the end of the world."

"In the first game," said Pippen, "we put a lot of pressure on ourselves."

Now the Bulls hope they can keep that pressure on the Lakers. ■

Faces on the Lakers' bench are as somber as the Game 2 final—107-86, Chicago.
PHOTO BY NANCY STONE

'They just caught fire.
They plain ol' whipped us.'
-Magic Johnson

7:47 – TIME TO FLY

Michael Jordan has had a virtual copyright on the word "air" since touching down in the NBA seven years ago.

So perhaps it was appropriate that one of his greatest flights ever began with a departure time of 7:47, that being the digits showing on the Stadium scoreboard clock during the fourth quarter of Game 2.

The Bulls were putting the clamps on the Lakers, going on a 15-2 run that would seal the game's outcome and tie the series at one, when Jordan went up for what everyone thought would be another resounding dunk.

At the last possible moment, however, Jordan saw Sam Perkins blocking his path to the hoop. At the apex of his flight, he quickly brought the ball down with his right hand, cradling it for a split-second before switching the ball to his left hand. Then, from just left of the basket, he banked it in off the glass before the laws of gravity forced him back down to the planet Earth.

It was an awe-inspiring basket. "He did the impossible," said Johnson. "The unbelievable."

Jordan, as is his style, downplayed the moment.

"Sometimes with creativity," he said after the game, "you never know what's going to happen."

– PAUL SULLIVAN

Michael Jordan performs "The Move" and, later, is hauled in by Scottie Pippen.
PHOTOS BY ED WAGNER
AND NANCY STONE (RIGHT)

Game 2: Bulls 107, Lakers 86

LAKERS (86)	Min	FG-att	FT-att	Reb	Ast	Fls	Pts
Sam Perkins	35	4-8	2-2	6	0	2	11
James Worthy	40	9-17	5-6	5	1	1	24
Vlade Divac	41	7-11	2-2	5	5	2	16
Byron Scott	26	2-2	0-0	0	2	4	5
Magic Johnson	43	4-13	6-6	7	10	2	14
Mychal Thompson	10	0-3	0-0	0	0	1	0
A.C. Green	22	2-11	0-0	7	0	2	6
Terry Teagle	14	0-2	6-6	1	1	1	6
Larry Drew	5	2-4	0-0	1	0	0	4
Elden Campbell	4	0-2	0-0	2	0	0	0
Totals	**240**	**30-73**	**21-22**	**34**	**19**	**15**	**86**

Percentages: FG .411, FT .955. **Three-point goals:** 5-12, .417. **Team rebounds:** 5. **Blocked shots:** 2 (Divac, Campbell). **Turnovers:** 17 (Worthy 4, Johnson 4, Perkins 3, Divac 2, Teagle 2, Thompson, Campbell). **Steals:** 8 (Divac 3, Johnson 2, Scott, Green Campbell). **Technical fouls:** 1, illegal defense, 9:40, 4th quarter. **Flagrant fouls:** Scott, 8:05, 3rd quarter.

BULLS (107)	Min	FG-att	FT-att	Reb	Ast	Fls	Pts
Scottie Pippen	44	8-16	4-4	5	10	4	20
Horace Grant	40	10-13	0-0	5	1	1	20
Bill Cartwright	24	6-9	0-0	5	1	1	12
John Paxson	25	8-8	0-0	0	6	2	16
Michael Jordan	36	15-18	3-4	7	13	4	33
Cliif Levingston	22	0-2	0-0	1	2	4	0
Craig Hodges	11	1-6	0-0	1	0	1	2
Will Perdue	11	1-3	0-0	7	1	0	2
B.J. Armstrong	7	0-2	0-0	1	1	0	0
Scott Williams	15	1-1	0-0	3	0	2	2
Stacey King	3	0-3	0-0	1	0	1	0
Dennis Hopson	2	0-0	0-0	0	0	0	0
Totals	**240**	**50-81**	**7-8**	**36**	**35**	**20**	**107**

Percentages: FG .617, FT .875. **Three-point goals:** 0-5, .000. **Team rebounds:** 1. **Blocked shots:** 1 (Jordan). **Turnovers:** 14 (Pippen 5, Jordan 4, Cartwright 2, Grant, Perdue, King.) **Steals:** 10 (Grant 2, Cartwright 2, Jordan 2, Levingston 2, Pippen, Paxson). **Technical fouls:** None. **Illegal defense:** 1.

L.A. Lakers	23 20 26 17	—	86
CHICAGO BULLS	28 20 38 21	—	107

A: 18,676. T: 2:10. Officials: J. Kersey, M. Mathis, J. O'Donnell.

OVERWHELMING IN OVERTIME

hen the Lakers' last, desperate, hopeless shot finally floated down to Michael Jordan, he cradled the ball in one hand and with his other hammered the floor in defiant triumph. Like hammering another nail into the

Lakers' coffin? Could be that's what the Bulls did with their thrilling 104-96 overtime victory in Game 3 of the NBA Finals.

As the Bulls prepared for Game 4 here June 9, they knew they had wrestled back the home-court advantage they lost in Game 1 and perhaps taken the Lakers' best shot along with a 2-1 series lead.

"We can never underestimate this team," said Michael Jordan, who scored 29 points, including a 14-foot jumper with 3.4 seconds left that sent the game into overtime and six points in the extra period. "But we did take a good shot. They extended the lead in the third quarter [going ahead by 13], but we were able to fight back and win.

"It will be tough for them to swallow, mentally, because they have to feel they gave one away."

This was to be a Lakers coronation before an adoring throng in the Forum. Magic Johnson was electric in scoring 22 points and handing off for 10 more baskets. Sam Perkins had 25 points, and Vlade Divac was elusive in scoring 24 before fouling out in overtime.

But the Bulls left the Lakers walking out with a sag in their shoulders and an emptiness in their eyes.

"We just didn't hit our shots," said Johnson. "And their offensive rebounds killed us."

That was a tribute to Horace Grant, who had a career-equaling playoff high 22 points and 11 rebounds, and Scottie Pippen, who had 19 points and

By Sam Smith

tied a career playoff high with 13 rebounds before fouling out late in regulation.

"I had talked to Horace going into the last game," said Pippen, "and we made a conscious effort to keep moving, to screen each other's man so we could get to the boards and get the second shots."

And it was big, the Bulls outrebounding L.A. 46-29, including a 16-9 advantage in offensive boards. The Lakers' 29 rebounds were an all-time low for the Finals.

But in the end it would come down to Jordan, who suffered a mild sprain of his right big toe on the last shot of regulation.

"It's sore," said Jordan, who will play Sunday. "I landed wrong. But I made the shot."

And it enabled the Bulls to send the game into overtime after a thrilling game that sent fans traveling from peaks of hope to valleys of despair.

The Bulls had come charging back against overwhelming odds after the Lakers' 18-2 run in the third quarter had given them a 67-54 lead.

After that, Cliff Levingston came through with his finest performance of the year, picking up a steal, a block, two key rebounds and a tip-in on the way to 10 points to give the Bulls' bench an 18-6 scoring margin over the Laker reserves.

"I was just trying to do some things to help change momentum," said Levingston. "L.A. was starting to make another surge, and we needed something."

Levingston capped his burst with a tip-in to give the

Scottie Pippen and Horace Grant sneak off the Forum floor after stealing Game 3.
PHOTO BY CHARLES CHERNEY

Bulls an 88-84 lead with 3:10 left in regulation.

"They were killing us on the boards," said Divac, "and that's why they won."

With his team trailing 92-90 with 10.9 seconds left, Bulls coach Phil Jackson elected to take possession at the far end of the court so Jordan could get a good look as he took the ball up.

"It's a time you concentrate more," said Jordan. His shot dropped like a stone and silenced the crowd. Jordan then slapped away the inbounds pass, and the Lakers were unable to get off a good last shot.

Now all the Bulls had to do was win in overtime for the first time all season.

Jordan drove and put in a reverse layup for a 98-96 lead. Perkins then missed and Jordan drove again. He missed, but Grant put back in the rebound for a 100-96 lead with 1:21 left in the overtime.

"I had gotten embarrassed in the first game, and I didn't want that to happen again," said Grant.

Perkins missed again, Levingston grabbing the rebound. Then Jordan drove, was fouled and hit two free throws to seal the victory, although Grant added a final jumper.

"We wanted to come in and get one win to take it back to Chicago," said Jordan. "But now we've got a good opportunity to win a couple more games." ■

TOAST ON THE COAST

The Bulls turned up the heat on the Lakers in Game 4. That's right, they cooked them. The Lakers were well-done after the 97-82 Bulls' win. Stick a fork in 'em. They're toast. "We can taste it," said Horace Grant. That's because the Bulls served up a delicious effort, taking an almost insurmountable 3-1 series lead with an all-out effort on both ends of the floor. The Lakers' 82 points marked the 14th time in 16 playoff games the Bulls held a team under 100 points.

Game 3: Bulls 104, Lakers 96 (OT)

BULLS (104)	Min	FG-att	FT-att	Reb	Ast	Fls	Pts
Horace Grant	42	9-11	4-4	11	3	2	22
Scottie Pippen	45	8-17	3-4	13	5	6	19
Bill Cartwright	33	2-8	2-2	3	1	3	6
Michael Jordan	52	11-28	6-6	9	9	5	29
John Paxson	36	5-11	0-0	0	3	1	10
Will Perdue	6	0-0	0-0	1	0	1	0
Craig Hodges	8	1-3	0-0	1	0	0	2
Cliff Levingston	20	5-5	0-0	4	0	1	10
B.J. Armstrong	9	0-1	0-0	2	0	0	0
Scott Williams	11	0-1	4-6	2	2	1	4
Stacey King	3	0-0	2-2	0	0	1	2
Totals	**265**	**41-85**	**21-24**	**46**	**23**	**21**	**104**

Percentages: FG .482, FT .875. **Three-point goals**: 1-3, .333 (Jordan 1-1, Pippen 0-1, Paxson 0-1). **Team rebounds**: 11. **Blocked shots**: 5 (Levingston 3, Jordan 2). **Turnovers**: 16 (Grant 5, Cartwright 4, Pippen 3, Jordan 3, Perdue). **Steals**: 10 (Pippen 4, Jordan 4, Grant, Levingston). **Technical fouls**: Pippen, :31 , 2nd quarter. **Illegal defense**: None.

LAKERS (96)	Min	FG-att	FT-att	Reb	Ast	Fls	Pts
Sam Perkins	51	10-17	5-6	9	2	3	25
James Worthy	48	9-16	1-2	1	4	1	19
Vlade Divac	41	11-15	2-2	7	0	6	24
Magic Johnson	50	7-15	8-9	6	10	2	22
Byron Scott	43	0-8	0-2	1	3	3	0
Terry Teagle	11	1-2	0-2	0	0	2	2
A.C. Green	15	1-3	0-2	4	0	2	2
Larry Drew	4	0-1	0-0	1	0	0	0
Elden Campbell	2	1-2	0-0	0	0	1	2
Totals	**265**	**40-79**	**16-25**	**29**	**19**	**20**	**96**

Percentages: FG .506, FT .640. **Three-point goals**: 0-8, .000 (Drew 0-1, Worthy 0-2, Johnson 0-2, Scott 0-3). **Team rebounds**: 9. **Blocked shots**: 7 (Perkins 5, Divac, Teagle). **Turnovers**: 14 (Johnson 5, Perkins 3, Divac 2, Scott 2, Worthy, Green). **Steals**: 9 (Worthy 3, Divac 2, Johnson 2, Perkins, Teagle). **Technical fouls**: None. **Illegal defense**: None.

CHICAGO BULLS	25	23	18	26	12 —104
L.A. Lakers	25	22	25	20	4 —96

A: 17,505. T: 2:50. Officials: D. Garretson, B. Oakes, J. Crawford.

Game 4: Bulls 97, Lakers 82

BULLS (97)	Min	FG-att	FT-att	Reb	Ast	Fls	Pts
Horace Grant	36	6-14	2-2	7	3	3	14
Scottie Pippen	40	6-12	2-2	9	6	4	14
Bill Cartwright	36	5-10	2-4	5	1	1	12
Michael Jordan	44	11-20	6-6	5	13	3	28
John Paxson	35	7-11	0-0	3	2	1	15
Cliff Levingston	20	2-3	0-0	5	0	3	4
Scott Williams	11	1-2	0-0	3	1	4	2
Craig Hodges	14	3-7	0-0	1	1	3	6
B.J. Armstrong	3	1-1	0-0	0	0	0	2
Will Perdue	1	0-0	0-0	0	0	0	0
Totals	**240**	**42-80**	**12-14**	**38**	**27**	**22**	**97**

Percentages: FG .525, FT .857. **Three-point goals**: 1-3, .333 (Paxson 1-2, Jordan 0-1). **Team rebounds**: 6. **Blocked shots**: 8 (Pippen 2, Cartwright 2, Jordan 2, Grant, Levingston). **Turnovers**: 5 (Pippen 2, Jordan, Paxson, Hodges). **Steals**: 4 (Grant 2, Pippen, Paxson). **Technical fouls**: None. **Illegal defense**: 1.

LAKERS (82)	Min	FG-att	FT-att	Reb	Ast	Fls	Pts
Sam Perkins	43	1-15	1-2	10	0	5	3
James Worthy	31	6-16	0-1	3	2	2	12
Vlade Divac	45	12-20	3-3	11	1	4	27
Magic Johnson	44	6-13	10-10	6	11	4	22
Byron Scott	34	2-4	0-0	4	0	5	4
A.C. Green	17	1-5	3-4	7	0	1	5
Terry Teagle	18	1-6	4-4	0	0	1	6
Larry Drew	6	1-2	1-2	0	0	1	3
Tony Smith	2	0-1	0-0	1	0	0	0
Totals	**240**	**30-82**	**22-26**	**42**	**14**	**23**	**82**

Percentages: FG .366, FT .846. **Three-point goals**: 0-5, .000 (Johnson 0-2, Perkins 0-3). **Team rebounds**: 10. **Blocked shots**: 3 (Divac 3). **Turnovers**: 9 (Divac 2, Johnson 2, Scott 2, Green 2, Smith). **Steals**: 4 (Teagle 2, Divac, Scott). **Technical fouls**: None. **Illegal defense**: None.

CHICAGO BULLS	27	25	22	23 —97
L.A. Lakers	28	16	14	24 —82

A: 17,505. T: 2:19. Officials: H. Evans, E. Rush, D. Bavetta.

Magic Johnson knows the Lakers' hopes are fading.
PHOTO BY JIM PRISCHING

Scottie Pippen hugs John Paxson during Game 4 (above).
PHOTO BY CHARLES CHERNEY

Paxson takes Laker guard Byron Scott's best shot.
PHOTO BY CHARLES CHERNEY

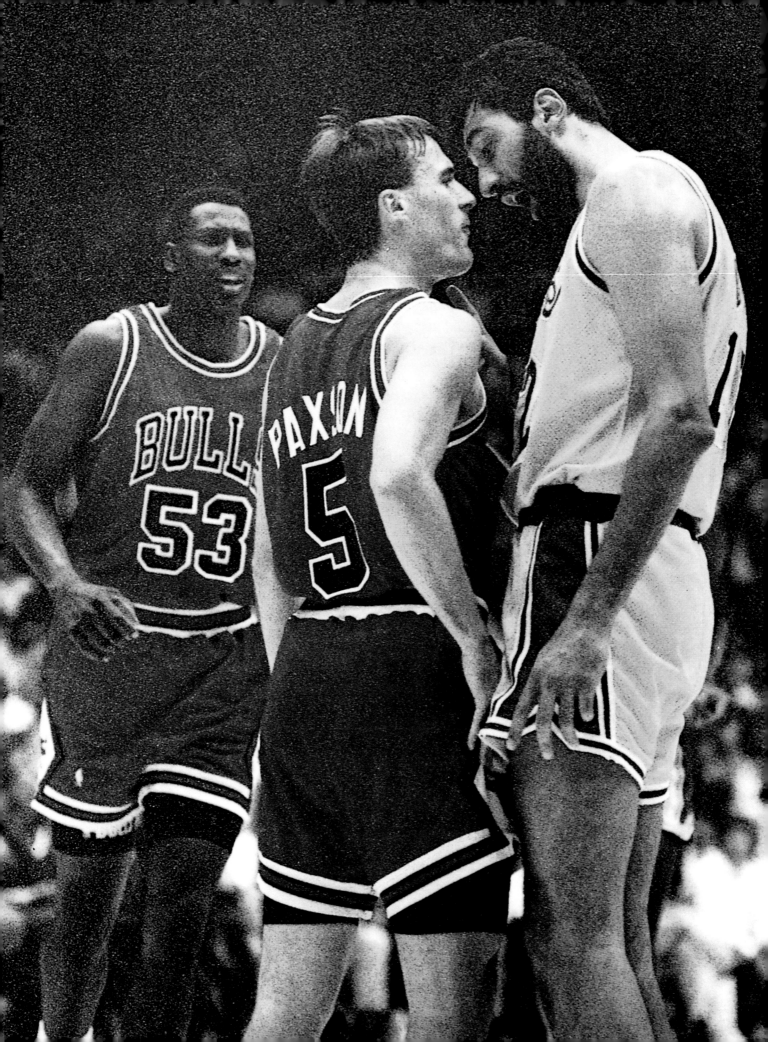

BULLS STAND TALL IN NBA FINALE

hampions!

"I never lost hope," said a tear-stained Michael Jordan, whose 30 points and 10 assists helped the Bulls wrap up their first NBA title June 12 with a thrilling 108-101 victory over the Los Angeles Lakers. "I'm so happy for my family and this team and this franchise. It's something I've worked seven years for, and I thank God for the talent and the opportunity that I've had."

Champions!

"I'm just happy for everyone, all of us—the organization, the city, the people of Chicago," said John Paxson, whose 20 points included 10 in a crucial three-minute stretch late in the fourth quarter after the Lakers had tied the score at 93. "It's an unbelievable feeling because we did it as a team. I can't wait to get home and share this with the city."

Champions!

"Pax was the key," said Bulls coach Phil Jackson. "M.J. was finding him and he stepped up and hit the shot."

"That's why I've always wanted him on my team and why I want him to stay on my team," said Jordan, holding the Larry O'Brien championship trophy while flanked by his wife, Juanita, and father, James, in the gleeful Bulls' locker room.

"I've never seen a celebration like this," said Jackson, drenched in champagne and the warmth of success. "I was with the '70 Knicks and the '73 Knicks, and there was never anything like this. This has been a

John Paxson fends off Vlade Divac during the Bulls' title-clinching win.
PHOTO BY JIM PRISCHING

By Sam Smith

poised team and they just lost it."

Champions!

They almost lost the game. The Lakers—led by Magic Johnson's 16 points, 20 assists and 11 rebounds and Elden Campbell's 21 points—made it difficult all the way for the Bulls.

But this was not a Bulls team to be denied, as they won the last four games—including all three at the Forum—to win the series 4-1.

Champions!

"We were fortunate and we were destined," said Jackson.

The Bulls plowed through the playoffs with a 15-2 record (an amazing 7-1 on the road), second best in NBA playoff history. They became the second team in the modern NBA era to win the title with the league's leading scorer on the team. They set five-game Finals records for best shooting, 52.7 percent; best defense, allowing only 91.6 points per game; most assists and steals; fewest turnovers and holding the opposition to the fewest rebounds.

They became the team of the '90s.

Champions!

"It's going to taste sweet for them," said Johnson, who came into the joyous Bulls' locker room to congratulate Jordan.

Rock breaks scissors and Air does ground Magic. The Lakers, without the injured James Worthy and Byron Scott, fought like aging champions, throwing

blow after blow at the Bulls.

The Lakers stormed the backboards early in taking a 49-48 halftime lead. But it would not be enough.

"We just couldn't overcome the loss of Worthy," said Johnson, who played the full 48 minutes. So did Jordan and Scottie Pippen, who led the Bulls in scoring with 32 points, the first time a player other than Jordan has been the Bulls' leading scorer in the playoffs.

" They made every big shot, Paxson in particular," said Johnson.

Champions!

Paxson gave the Bulls a lead they would never surrender with a 19-foot jumper. Then, after a Sam Perkins jumper fell short, Jordan found Paxson for an 18-footer.

"It was a tribute to Michael finding the open man like that," said Jackson.

Perkins, who led the Lakers with 22 points, missed a three-pointer and Paxson took a pass from Pippen and drove for a 99-93 Bulls lead with three minutes left.

"It seemed like Paxson never missed a shot in this series," said Perkins about Paxson's 65 percent marksmanship against the Lakers.

The Lakers would make one last run, closing within 103-101 when Perkins converted a three-point play with 1:13 left.

But back came Paxson, hitting nothing but bottom from 18 feet for a 105-101 lead with :56 left. The Lakers wouldn't score again.

Champions!

And they exulted.

Pippen, who also had a playoff-high 13 rebounds, popped the first champagne bottle as the team came sprinting into the locker room, dumping the bubbly over a bubbling Horace Grant as the locker room resembled a fraternity party.

"We're going to celebrate for at least two days," said Pippen.

The players immediately gathered in a circle for a prayer and then grabbed champagne bottles, dousing one another, Bill Cartwright quietly saying "Finally," and Paxson running up for the trophy presentation

Scottie Pippen begins to celebrate during the waning seconds of Game 5 in L.A. Photo By Jim Prisching

from Commissioner David Stern.

"I've got to be a part of this," he yelled.

Bulls owner Jerry Reinsdorf smiled and laughed and wore champagne like a comfortable suit.

Champions!

General Manager Jerry Krause hugged Craig Hodges. Hodges lived.

"It doesn't get any better than this," said Hodges.

Championship hats and T-shirts were distributed. June Jackson looked for husband Phil; Donna Grant for husband Horace. Everyone screamed and hugged.

Champions!

Will Perdue dumped champagne on Cartwright, and Hodges stood alone, shouting, "Yeah, yeah, yeah!"

Champions!

For a long time, Jordan sat along one of the long benches in the visitors' locker room. In many ways, it was his party.

He hid his head in the arms of his wife for a long time after receiving the MVP trophy and cried.

Finally, he picked up his head as reporters and photographers gathered in a tightening circle.

His eyes were red and tears glistened on his cheeks, reflecting in the lights. It could have been champagne, but it wasn't.

"I never showed this kind of emotion before in public," he apologized.

He didn't have to. He really is human. For years, he's threatened and cajoled, been praised as the best example of team basketball and villified as the worst example. He basked in the spotlight put on him, but was also cursed by it. Could he be a winner?

"We started from scratch, on the bottom, not making the playoffs when I got here," said Jordan. "It took seven years, but we won. This should get rid of the stigma of the one-man team. We have players that make us an effective basketball team."

All champions! ■

Game 5: Bulls 108, Lakers 101

BULLS (108)	Min	FG-att	FT-att	Reb	Ast	Fls	Pts
Horace Grant	40	4-5	3-6	6	0	2	11
Scottie Pippen	48	10-22	11-12	13	7	3	32
Bill Cartwright	33	4-11	0-0	8	7	5	8
Michael Jordan	48	12-23	6-8	4	10	1	30
John Paxson	33	9-12	2-2	3	4	3	20
Cliff Levingston	8	0-1	0-0	2	0	4	0
Scott Williams	7	2-2	0-0	0	0	0	5
Craig Hodges	8	0-0	0-0	1	0	2	0
B.J. Armstrong	8	1-2	0-0	0	0	0	2
Will Perdue	7	0-0	0-0	0	0	3	0
Totals	**240**	**42-78**	**22-28**	**37**	**28**	**23**	**108**

Percentages: FG .538, FT .786. **Three-point goals**: 2-3, .667 (Hodges 1-1, Pippen 1-2). **Team rebounds**: 6. **Blocked shots**: 6 (Grant 2, Jordan 2, Pippen, Williams). **Turnovers**: 18 (Pippen 7, Jordan 6, Grant 2, Paxson, Armstrong, Perdue). **Steals**: 14 (Jordan 5, Pippen 5, Grant, Cartwright, Armstrong, Paxson). **Technical fouls**: None. **Illegal defense**: 1.

LAKERS (101)	Min	FG-att	FT-att	Reb	Ast	Fls	Pts
A.C. Green	43	6-12	1-2	7	1	3	13
Sam Perkins	37	5-12	11-13	9	3	4	22
Vlade Divac	37	4-12	0-0	7	3	2	8
Magic Johnson	48	4-12	6-6	11	20	0	16
Terry Teagle	18	4-8	1-2	0	0	4	9
Elden Campbell	27	9-12	3-4	2	0	3	21
Tony Smith	30	5-6	2-3	0	2	6	12
Totals	**240**	**37-74**	**24-30**	**36**	**29**	**22**	**101**

Percentages: FG .500, FT .800. **Three-point goals**: 3-11, .273 (Johnson 2-6, Perkins 1-4, Divac 0-1). **Team rebounds**: 6. **Blocked shots**: 7 (Divac 4, Perkins 2, Campbell). **Turnovers**: 22 (Johnson 6, Divac 5, Smith 4, Teagle 3, Green 2, Perkins, Campbell). **Steals**: 6 (Green 2, Campbell, Johnson, Smith). **Technical fouls**: None. **Flagrant fouls**: 1 (Perkins). **Illegal defense**: None.

CHICAGO BULLS		27 21 32 28	—108
L.A. Lakers		25 24 31 21	—101

A: 17,505. T: 2:28. Officials: J. O'Donnell, J. Madden, M. Mathis.

Finals composite box: Bulls vs. Lakers

BULLS (4-1)	G	Avg min	FG pct	FT pct	Reb	Ast	Avg pts
Jordan	5	44.0	.556	.848	33	57	31.2
Pippen	5	43.6	.453	.862	47	33	20.8
Grant	5	38.0	.627	.750	39	8	14.6
Paxson	5	31.8	.653	1.000	10	17	13.4
Cartwright	5	32.0	.435	.667	25	12	8.8
Levingston	5	18.0	.615	–	14	3	3.2
Hodges	5	10.6	.391	–	3	1	3.8
Williams	5	9.0	.400	.667	9	3	1.6
Perdue	5	7.5	.600	1.000	12	1	1.6
Armstrong	5	7.4	.455	–	3	4	2.0
King	2	3.0	.000	1.000	1	0	0.4
Hopson	1	2.0	–	–	0	0	0.0
Totals	**5**	**–**	**.527**	**.848**	**196**	**139**	**101.4**

Three-point goals: 5-21, .238 (Jordan 2-4, Pippen 1-5, Hodges 1-6, Paxson 0-3, Armstrong 0-1, King 0-1). **Team rebounds**: 30. **Blocked shots**: 25. **Turnovers**: 63. **Steals**: 50. **Technical fouls**: None. **Illegal defense**: 3. **Flagrant fouls**: None.

LAKERS (1-4)	G	Avg min	FG pct	FT pct	Reb	Ast	Avg pts
Worthy	4	41.0	.479	.667	12	8	19.3
Johnson	5	45.6	.431	.951	40	62	18.6
Divac	5	41.6	.565	1.000	44	10	18.2
Perkins	5	41.2	.405	.759	38	5	16.6
Green	5	22.6	.294	.583	28	1	7.6
Scott	4	35.0	.277	.700	7	7	4.5
Teagle	5	14.2	.333	.786	2	1	5.0
Drew	4	5.0	.375	.500	2	0	1.8
Campbell	3	11.0	.625	.750	4	0	3.7
Thompson	1	10.0	.000	–	0	0	0.0
Smith	1	30.0	.833	.666	0	2	12.0
Totals	**5**	**–**	**.447**	**.810**	**178**	**106**	**81.6**

Three-point goals: 13-46 .283 (Perkins 5-13, Johnson 4-14, Green 2-3, Scott 1-5, Worthy 1-6, Divac 0-2, Drew 0-4). **Team rebounds**: 36. **Blocked shots**: 22. **Turnovers**: 75. **Steals**: 34. **Technical fouls**: None. **Illegal defense**: 1. **Flagrant fouls**: 2.

Chicago Tribune

Thursday, June 13, 1991   35¢

NBA Championship Final

High five! Bulls are champs!

Bulls
108
Lakers
101

Jordan soars: For the first time in 17 playoff games, Michael Jordan didn't lead Bulls' scorers. But his team's night was still tops. **In Sports.**

Big shot: The Bulls "other" guard, John Paxson, was 32 of 49 from the field, shooting 65 percent against the Lakers. **In Sports.**

Saying thanks: Reserve Craig Hodges led his teammates in a postgame prayer while national television cameras rolled. **In Sports.**

"[The championship] means so much. Not just for me but for this team and this city. It was a seven-year struggle. It's the most proud day I've ever had."

Michael Jordan, in tears, after the Bulls' victory

Tribune photo by Charles Cherney

Michael Jordan, alone with his thoughts in a jubilant Bulls locker room, clutches the championship trophy that eluded him for six seasons—and Chicago for 25.

1st title sweeps away 25 years of frustration

By Sam Smith
Chicago Tribune

INGLEWOOD, Calif.—All this started with New York, almost two months ago and, fittingly, ends with Los Angeles.

The Bulls have swept across the National Basketball Association landscape in a remarkable cross-country run to the title that has left no doubt about the location of the basketball capital of the world.

Chicago is second to none.

"[The championship] means so much," said Michael Jordan, in tears after the game talking to a national television audience. "Not just for me but for this team and this city. It was a seven-year struggle. It's the most proud day I've ever had."

Jordan was named Most Valuable Player of the NBA Finals, which the Bulls won 4 games to one—including three straight on the road in Los Angeles.

Yes, the Bulls have taken the gold in their silver anniversary season, a tempest of effort finally sending the proud Lakers sinking into the Pacific Wednesday night in a hard-fought 108-101 game and letting loose a tidal wave of exhilaration and emotion.

The Bulls are champions!

Roll it around in your mouth and savor the sweet taste of victory. Close your eyes and see them raising the banners in honor of the Bulls, in honor of all Bulls teams and, really, in honor of all Chicagoans. Get ready for Friday's noon rally at the Petrillo Band Shell in Grant Park.

Because the Bulls have been Chicago's team, winning with a bit of Gold Coast glamor and a lot of stockyards effort.

This not only has been an inexorable march to glory, it has been a 100-yard dash to success. The Bulls sped through the playoffs with a 15-2 record, equaling the best since the NBA went to the current postseason format and posting the second-best all-time playoff winning percentage.

The Bulls did it with some of the best marksmanship an NBA Finals has seen and a suffocating defense that broke records for fewest points scored by their opponents, yet they refused to allow the beauty and grace of the game to be diminished.

Jordan, with 30 points and 10 assists Wednesday night, danced on air. Scottie Pippen, who tallied a

See **Champions**, pg. 16

This time the waiting isn't until next year

For 1 special night, everyone's a fan

By Charles Leroux
and Charles M. Madigan

Before Chicago erupted into a late-night shout, a thumbs-up, triumphant, "YES," before the Bulls' 108-101 victory over the Los Angeles Lakers, before fans spilled cheering into the streets and fireworks crackled and car horns honked in glee, there was the wait.

You found Chicago fans in the strangest places during the game Wednesday night, waiting for the Bulls to take the National Basketball Associaton championship. And for some of them, it seemed nothing could get in the way of watching the battle with the Los Angeles Lakers.

At Hinsdale Hospital, in one class on natural childbirth, seven pregnant women and their husbands ate cookies colored and shaped like basketballs. Some of them had snapshots taken beside a full-sized cutout of Michael Jordan.

In another classroom, a TV displayed the game without sound while teacher Nadine Thornton instructed men on how to coach their wives during labor. Learning how to breath properly helps with having babies, and with watching the Bulls too.

"I take a cleansing breath every time Michael Jordan throws up a shot," said Renee Sipek, 32, of Westmont, who is in the 8th month of her pregnancy. She inhaled deeply and exhaled to demonstrate.

"It didn't even hurt," she said.

In one of the hospital's operating rooms, an anesthesiologist placed a small television set into the far corner of an operating room where a woman was undergoing a bowel resection.

The doctor "assured the patient that 'We'll take real good care of you despite the fact that we have the Bulls game on,'" according to one of the night nurses.

In the birthing room at the hospital, Donald Porter, 40, was with his wife, Shirley, 32, as she was working through labor. Their first child, they had already learned, would be a daughter.

"I bought her a Bulls T-shirt already. I hope the Bulls take this tonight. So I can always remember her birthday."

●●●

There was no parking problem at Chicago Stadium Wednesday night.

Michael Scott, 26, of Cicero, and a dozen friends and family members gathered around his Bulls-red Chevy Blazer to watch the game on a TV perched on the hood. They were the sole occupants of the vast parking lot.

"We wanted to celebrate at the stadium," Scott said. "So we took

See **The wait**, pg. 18

■ Fans throw impromptu parties; some get out of hand. Page 16.

How the Bulls won the title

Tribune photos by Jim Prisching, Charles Cherney

1 Michael Jordan. Enough said.

2 Development of Scottie Pippen and Horace Grant. Pippen now has star status; Grant was a key man in playoffs.

3 Defense. Team committed to executing a high-intensity defensive pressure system.

4 Phil Jackson. The second-year coach exuded a calming influence on an excitable team.

5 No major injuries to starters. Jordan, Pippen, John Paxson played every game. Grant missed 4; Bill Cartwright sat out 3.

Bulls win respect for themselves and their town

By Bernie Lincicome
Chicago Tribune

INGLEWOOD, Calif.—Respect.

This has been about respect from the beginning, from the time Michael Jordan first arrived in Chicago, an Olympic hero and an infant conglomerate, to the dawn of this day, the day the Bulls are champions of basketball.

Respect for Jordan, who has to imagine more critics than he has in order to reach ever higher.

"Ten years ago," Jordan said, "I was just a kid scared to death, leaving high school, won-

Commentary

dering if I could play at the next level.

"Now, 10 years later, I'm at the highest level."

The nagging accusations of ego and selfishness against Jordan no longer have a voice, for this is a trophy with the fingerprints of an entire team on it.

Genius is, by its nature, selfish, but invaluable to anyone wise enough to use it properly. Genius can carry heavy loads to where it must go.

"Ten years down the road, no one would ever remember Michael Jordan, the challenger," said Jordan, the champion.

This is about respect for the Bulls, a team so obscured by Jordan it must fight its own invisibility.

"Thank you for asking me a question," said John Paxson, seated next to Jordan in one of the media sessions.

This is about respect for a bumbling franchise, a quarter of a century into alibis, a franchise that can consider the luckiest day in its history the day that Houston selected Hakeem

See **Respect**, pg. 16

Anti-Semitic outbreak stains Leningrad election

By Thom Shanker
Chicago Tribune

LENINGRAD—As residents in this most European of Russian cities voted Wednesday whether to restore its historic name, St. Petersburg, an outbreak of virulent anti-Semitism proved that Leningrad also remains the most xenophobically Russian of Soviet cities.

Just hours before the polls opened, a wall along an entire block of Nevsky Prospect, Leningrad's main thoroughfare, was covered with posters crudely depicting hook-nosed Jews.

They alleged a Zionist conspiracy—behind the centrist reforms of Soviet President Mikhail Gorbachev, behind the radical platform of Boris Yeltsin, who is seeking the presidency of the Russian Republic and even behind the idea of dropping the communist-era name of Leningrad.

One, for example, was a particu-

■ Yeltsin the likely new leader of the Russian Republic. Page 20.

larly nasty caricature of a member of the Rothschild financial dynasty. The individual was pulling puppet strings to control Gorbachev and Yeltsin.

Another, put up by Vladimir Fursov, a leader of Leningrad's "Fatherland" society, depicted a Nazi mapmaker trying to erase Leningrad in 1941.

Beneath it was a drawing of a ballot used in Wednesday's voting, leaving the clear impression that voters opting for a return of the name St. Petersburg were as intent on destroying the city as Hitler's Wehrmacht.

Although the site has become Leningrad's Speakers Corner, open to appeals for all causes, a cell of right-wing fanatics forcefully ejected a Yeltsin supporter seeking to

See **Name**, pg. 20

Thursday

Road trips: Memories of summers past include dream-like visions of beaches, faraway cities and pretty towns. But, when families traveled by car, getting there could be a nightmare. **In Tempo.**

Kitchen crusaders: The most obvious and easiest place to start a recycling revolution of your own is in the kitchen. Some tips, **in Food Guide.**

Weather

Chicago and vicinity: Thursday: Mostly sunny; high 82 degrees. Thursday night: Partly cloudy, chance for late storms; low 64. Friday: Cloudy, humid, chance for storms; high 89. The national weather report is in **Sec. 2, pg. 7.**

Schwarzkopf: Expand combat role for women

By Elaine S. Povich
Chicago Tribune

WASHINGTON—Moving out in front of many military leaders, Gen. H. Norman Schwarzkopf said Wednesday that the role of women in combat should be expanded, but not to the point of fighting in infantry units.

Setting the stage for upcoming Senate votes on permitting the armed services to assign women to combat roles, Schwarzkopf said the current line separating women from all combat participation has to be moved. But he refused to say if he favored allowing women to fly Navy and Air Force combat missions, a step already taken by the House.

The Senate Armed Services Committee, where America's best-known combat general was testifying Wednesday, will take up the

Tribune photo by Ernie Cox Jr.

Gen. Norman Schwarzkopf testifies before a Senate panel.

issue of women in air combat shortly. Under current law, women can fly transport and tanker planes and serve on crews of repair and supply ships.

But women are not assigned to combat aircraft or ships. The Army also has a policy barring women from direct combat roles.

The invasion force that Schwarzkopf led into the desert

See **Women**, pg. 20

Chicago Tribune
Sports

Section 4 ★   Thursday, June 13, 1991

NBA Finals: Chicago vs. L.A.

Phil Jackson, whose poise is so evident as Bulls coach, and Michael Jordan, always in command on the court, are washed out of character by a champagne shower during the championship celebration.
Tribune photo by Charles Cherney

Bulls stampede to first title

Bernie Lincicome
In the wake of the news

These champions did it with style

Chicago Tribune

INGLEWOOD, Calif.—Coming home. Coming home champions.

Michael Jordan's feet knew it with 10 seconds to play. His feet wanted to skip, wanted to leap, wanted to do anything but follow his dribble up the floor.

Jordan's hands wanted to applaud, wanted to hug somebody, wanted to do anything but shoot one more meaningless foul shot.

And when it was official, when it was indelible, when the Bulls had taken the Lakers in five, had brought from the coast the first basketball trophy for Chicago, Jordan's hands and feet and celebrated tongue did what they needed to do, leap and hug and shout.

Champions.

Jack Nicholson, the celebrity symbol of the team of celebrities, hugged Phil Jackson, the coach of the team from the city of big shoulders. Magic Johnson found his way through the grim despair of losing friends to congratulate the beaming Jordan.

"I saw tears in his eyes," Johnson said. "I told him, 'You proved everyone wrong. You're a winner as well as a great individual basketball player.'"

Jordan hugged Cliff Levingston. Horace Grant hugged Scottie Pippen.

And across the land, over the mountains, from great ocean to Great Lake, the warmth of a basketball team embraced a city.

"Chicago will love this," promised Johnson.

For all its championship seasons, so few, so distant, Chicago can savor this one. It came without surprise or excuse or great dispute.

It came without surprise or excuse or great dispute.

The Bulls spent a season earning the right to do the expected, never a forgiving reward. And then they did even better than expected, sweeping the Knicks and Pistons, coming within two late three-point shots of sweeping the 76ers and the Lakers.

"This is something," Jordan said, choking on his words. "This is a seven-year struggle for me, for the city. When I came here, we started from scratch, from the bottom.

"Each year, we got closer and closer. We plugged and plugged, and the light was still

See Lincicome, pg. 5

With Scottie Pippen soaring above him, the Lakers' Vlade Divac finds the ball squirting away. Divac scored only eight points.
Tribune photo by Jim Prisching

Jordan, Paxson oust Lakers

By Sam Smith
Chicago Tribune

INGLEWOOD, Calif.—Champions!

"I never lost hope," said a tear-stained Michael Jordan, whose 30 points and 10 assists helped the Bulls wrap up their first NBA title Wednesday with a thrilling 108-101 victory over the Los Angeles Lakers. "I'm so happy for my family and this team and this franchise. It's something I've worked seven years for, and I thank God for the talent and the opportunity that I've had."

Champions!

"I'm just happy for everyone, all of us—the organization, the city, the people of Chicago," said John Paxson, whose 20 points

More Bulls coverage
■ Jerry Krause and his bench earn redemption. Page 4.
■ By Mayor Daley's order, Friday will be Bulls' day. Page 5.
■ New NBA champs' celebration a real ball. Back page.

included 10 in a crucial three-minute stretch late in the fourth quarter after the Lakers had tied the score at 93. "It's an unbelievable feeling because we did it as a team. I can't wait to get home and share this with the city."

Champions!

"Pax was the key," said Bulls coach Phil Jackson. "M.J. was finding him and he stepped up and hit the shot."

"That's why I've always wanted him on my team and why I want him to stay on my team," said Jordan, holding the Larry O'Brien championship trophy while flanked by his wife, Juanita, and father, James, in the gleeful Bulls locker room.

"I've never seen a celebration like this," said Jackson, drenched in champagne and the warmth of success. "I was with the '70 Knicks and the '73 Knicks, and there was never anything like this. This has been a poised team and they just lost it."

Champions!

They almost lost the game. The Lakers—led by Magic Johnson's 16 points, 20 assists and 11 rebounds and Elden Campbell's 21

See Bulls, pg. 5

Even Magic can't save L.A.

By Skip Myslenski
Chicago Tribune

INGLEWOOD, Calif.—The great ones acknowledge no limits and do not flinch, no matter the odds. The great ones are fueled by a fire that sears their belly, are laced with a tensile strength that refuses to bend, are buoyed by a confidence that convinces them they will, somehow, someway, find a way to prevail.

Magic Johnson is a great one, and on Wednesday night at the Forum, he proved this once again. He could not prevent the Bulls from winning their title,

could not pull the ragamuffin band surrounding him to a victory, yet over 48 resplendent minutes, he bared his will and his soul and every one of the considerable skills at his command.

He walked, when it ended, straight to the Bulls' locker room and there congratulated Michael Jordan and those others he had battled so tenaciously. He had hit them with 16 points, with 20 assists, with 11 rebounds, with countless feints from his deep bag of tricks, yet here he was telling Jordan, "Congratulations. You finally got what you want."

"It was a big moment," Johnson would say later. "He had been billed as an individual, and now he's proven all those people wrong. He had a remarkable year, both as an individual and a team [player]. He's the best, this year. It's going to be sweet for him. Swe-e-e-t. Unbelievable. It's going to be unreal."

Here, moments after defeat, Magic Johnson was again proving himself a great one, proving it as he had in the game so recently ended. He had played without forward James Worthy,

See Lakers, pg. 4

Living legend caps off a splendid 1990-91 season

By Paul Sullivan
Chicago Tribune

INGLEWOOD, Calif.—All in all, it was not a bad year for Michael Jordan.

He welcomed his second son into the world, had a hamburger named after him, won his fifth straight scoring title, agreed to let a network use his likeness in a Saturday morning cartoon, earned his second Most Valuable Player award, cut a commercial

with Little Richard, scored 21 points in one quarter, grabbed 19 rebounds in one game and hit a free throw with his eyes closed.

Oh, and one other thing.

He finally got the ring. The championship ring.

"I'm going to pass it on down to my kids," said an exuberant Jordan afterward. "No one can take it away from me. I don't know if I'll ever have this feeling

again. All the things I've gone through, all the things the city has gone through, it was a lot of hard work, and what you see is the emotions of all that hard work paying off."

Though Jordan scored 30 points on the night, adding 10 assists and five steals, he played second-fiddle to his sizzling backcourt mate, John Paxson. But Jordan still managed to cop the "Most Valuable Player trophy

for the NBA Finals.

"I could care less," he said of yet another individual honor. "The whole team is the MVP. The whole city is the MVP."

Befitting the Jordan legend, with a minute and a half left in the game, he threw up a blind shot over his shoulder from 10 feet out that went through the hoop. Though it came after a foul and did not count, it was a perfect shot to sum up a perfect

season.

The Jordan-led Bulls dominated to the last shot in 1990-91. From a last-second Nov. 21 loss at Phoenix that put them at 5-6, through Wednesday's thrilling wrap-up, the Bulls played at an .807 clip, going 71-17.

Jordan's playoff performance left him with a career playoff point total of 2,425, passing Bob Pettit for 15th-place on the all-

See Jordan, pg. 4

The sweat of an entire
season is washed away in
a champagne shower of
pure celebration.
PHOTO BY CHARLES CHERNEY

Tenacity, Trust and a First Title

Bernie Lincicome

IN THE WAKE OF THE NEWS

Coming home. Coming home champions.

Michael Jordan's feet knew it with 10 seconds to play. His feet wanted to skip, wanted to leap, wanted to do anything but follow his dribble up the floor.

Jordan's hands wanted to applaud, wanted to hug somebody, wanted to do anything but shoot one more meaningless foul shot.

And when it was official, when it was indelible, when the Bulls had taken the Lakers in five, had brought from the coast the first basketball trophy for Chicago, Jordan's hands and feet and celebrated tongue did what they needed to do, leap and hug and shout.

Champions.

Jack Nicholson, the celebrity symbol of the team of celebrities, hugged Phil Jackson, the coach of the team from the city of big shoulders. Magic Johnson found his way through the grim despair of losing friends to congratulate the beaming Jordan.

"I saw tears in his eyes," Johnson said. "I told him, 'You proved everyone wrong. You're a winner as well as a great individual basketball player.' "

Jordan hugged Cliff Levingston. Horace Grant hugged Scottie Pippen.

And across the land, over the mountains, from great ocean to Great Lake, the warmth of a basketball team embraced a city.

"Chicago will love this," promised Johnson.

For all its championship seasons, so few, so distant, Chicago can savor this one. It came with style and dignity and honest purpose.

It came without surprise or excuse or great dispute.

The Bulls spent a season earning the right to do the expected, never a forgiving reward. And then they did even better than expected, sweeping the Knicks and Pistons, coming within two late three-point shots of sweeping the 76ers and the Lakers.

"This is something," Jordan said, choking on his words. "This is a seven-year struggle for me, for the city. When I came here, we started from scratch, from the bottom.

"I've never been this emotional in public. But I don't mind."

Though the Lakers, the franchise of a generation, became the invalids of Inglewood, that only eased the way for the inevitable.

"The best team we played," said Lakers coach Mike Dunleavy, ending all arguments of what might have happened had the Bulls met Portland.

It was a Finals to take the breath away, an intersection of the greatest talents and personalities of the game, Magic Johnson and Michael Jordan.

Though this Magic Johnson was the used model, so discouraged by age and ordinariness that he hinted at retiring, though these Lakers were not those Lakers, none of this can taint the Bulls' achievement.

The Bulls may not have reinvented defense, but they returned it from the thugs to the athletes. They played defense with grace instead of cruelty, leaving more gasps than scars, a youthful, dashing, daring defense, requiring energy and cooperation.

"Tenacity and trust," said Jackson.

The Bulls proclaimed themselves a team when it was over, as if they had not been before. Of course, they were. They always have been. They just were not a good enough team.

"You dream about this," said John Paxson, whose stretch-shooting put away the Lakers finally and for good. "The best thing is, we did it as a team."

After 2,163 games, the Bulls have an NBA championship. After 644 games in the Michael Jordan era, the Bulls have an NBA championship.

"Maybe it will be our turn again next year," said Johnson.

Titles are hard to get. Harder to keep.

This is the first. ∎

Whether a Bulls' fan in Chicago...

...or a player in Los Angeles, the NBA title meant respect for the city.

PHOTOS BY MICHAEL FRYER (TOP) AND CHARLES CHERNEY.

A (CHICAGO!?) TEAM FOR THE AGES

ur proposition here is that Chicago loves the Bulls not only because of what they did but how they did it. They took the old sports cliche about "putting it all together" on a fast break and didn't pull up until an NBA championship was theirs.

We needn't recycle the sorry litany of failures past from other franchises in these parts. This city has been blessed with more great athletes than great teams. All too often, Chicago stars performed with athletes who barely deserved their stripes.

But the Bulls gave their fans everything they could have asked, and more. Basketball is the ultimate team game, with five players working for the best shot inside 24 seconds, then instantly reverting to defense for a counter-attack by the opposition.

By Bob Verdi

You can argue against NBA players as the best athletes in the world, but come prepared, because you'll probably lose. Magic Johnson performed at reduced efficiency—or was reduced by what the Bulls did—in the NBA Finals, and still he was everywhere.

NBA players all possess the obvious physical gifts, and in that respect, they are no different from counterparts leagues apart. But in no other game are athletes required to be so well-rounded; 12-man rosters tend to preclude specialists. Pitchers can't hit. Goalies can't stickhandle. Placekickers can't run a pass pattern. Yet even the most one-dimensional NBA player is capable of being at least respectable with his weakest skill, and the stamina of these physical specimens is beyond reproach.

So, then, if the game is unique, the team that masters it even for a single season, from November to June, stands to be special. The Bulls are, and have been. They started 0-3 and still promised that they would pull it together. Did they ever, and they did it as a team, as they had to to win. Moreover, the Bulls did it with probably the most talented individual, Michael

Jordan, in league history. Not since 1971 has the NBA's leading scorer also earned a championship ring. That says a lot about him and a lot about the Bulls.

Which is why Chicago couldn't help but attach itself to this team. Here is the best solo act ever, Jordan, and yet the Bulls complemented him as well as he did them. Defense means sacrifice, rebounding is hard work, diving for loose balls demands effort. Chicago, a city that likes to roll up its sleeves, adores Jordan. But the Bulls were the whole package, and we can't even accuse them of being the best team money can buy. On the pecking order of NBA payrolls, they rank 23rd. When John Paxson goes 8 for 8 from the floor, he isn't feeling sorry about his modest salary.

Of course, there isn't a team on the planet that doesn't complain about something, and the Bulls complied. Jordan asked for more help, Scottie Pippen for more money, and a couple others asked for more action. But then Phil Jackson, the long arm of the law, gathered his people, pulled the curtain on practice and coached his students toward their higher calling.

Jerry Reinsdorf, the owner, and Jerry Krause, the general manager, generally do not register high on popularity polls. But the former gets to go to the bank, anyway, and the latter gets the last laugh. Reinsdorf trusted Krause even when advised otherwise, and Krause trusted his instincts, even when no less a giant than Jordan questioned the squad's depth of talent.

Best of all, when the Bulls and their fans realized that this squad was just Michael Jordan and a bunch of names to be played apprehensively, the rest of the NBA waited for further evidence. Well, it's official now, from here to Hollywood. Yes, the best player won. But so did the best team. The Bulls proved that floor burns only hurt for a little while. ∎

Phil Jackson and the rest of the Bulls acknowledge the fans at O'Hare.
PHOTO BY MICHAEL FRYER

Police estimated the crowd for the Bulls' rally in Grant Park at 500,000. Others said one million. No matter the number, they all cheered as one for their World Champion Chicago Bulls. "We started from the bottom, and it was hard working our way to the top. But we did it," said Michael Jordan.

PHOTO BY GEORGE THOMPSON

THE WAIT IS OVER

Bernie Lincicome

IN THE WAKE OF THE NEWS

When Michael Jordan speaks of seven years as if it were a prison sentence, you think of Ernie Banks, who still is waiting, and of Walter Payton, who had a decade of lumps and then watched a fat tackle get his Super Bowl touchdown.

You wonder, where was Nellie Fox's World Series ring or Denis Savard's Stanley Cup souvenir?

You want to tell Jordan that this is a precious thing that has happened, a rare and wonderful thing, but you think he knows.

There was just too much damp joy and sweet relief from Jordan not to know, too much raw emotion from the man who is still more careful image than human being to the rest of us.

The Jordan of commerce is the one we know, exploiting and exaggerating his gifts for profit, flitting across the moon or leaping from product to merchandise, a comic-book Jordan, invincible and superhuman.

That is all fantasy; the tears were real.

Early in these playoffs—Philadelphia, I think—Jordan is trying to explain he is not ashamed of his career or of the mark he has made on either basketball or the marketplace, even if he doesn't get a championship.

He could walk away, he says, without regret.

Those tears of his that moistened the championship trophy were because he now knows he will not have to.

What you wish is that this had not meant so much to Jordan or to Chicago. What you wish for both a great player and a great city is that there would be a ninth championship opportunity so that the winning or the losing does not define things forever.

How much of a fool does one have to be not to have seen the first time Jordan stepped on the floor for the Bulls that this kite could soar and all that was neces-

Michael Jordan greets the fans at O'Hare after—finally—earning an NBA title.
PHOTO BY MICHAEL FRYER

sary was to give it the proper tail?

How many times did the Bulls start over in seven years? Four by my count. And what was the one constant in all those changes, the new coaches, the curious trades, the botched drafts?

Jordan.

At the Bulls' age, there ought to be three or four more of these, though the ingredients responsible for this one cannot, nor should not, be duplicated.

This one, like a first love, will always be special. ■

1991 Bulls playoff results

Home team all caps

First round: Bulls beat Knicks 3-0

Date	Score	Top Bulls scorer	Top rebounder
4/25	BULLS 126, Knicks 86	Jordan (29)	Grant (8)
4/28	BULLS 89, Knicks 79	Jordan (26)	Pippen (8)
4/30	Bulls 103, KNICKS 94	Jordan (33)	Pippen (11)

Second round: Bulls beat 76ers 4-1

Date	Score	Top Bulls scorer	Top rebounder
5/4	BULLS 105, 76ers 92	Jordan (29)	Grant (9)
5/6	BULLS 112, 76ers 100	Jordan (29)	Pippen (11)
5/10	76ERS 99, Bulls 97	Jordan (46)	Pippen (13)
5/12	Bulls 101, 76ERS 85	Jordan (25)	Grant (11)
5/14	BULLS 100, 76ers 95	Jordan (38)	Jordan (19)

Conference finals: Bulls beat Pistons 4-0

Date	Score	Top Bulls scorer	Top rebounder
5/19	BULLS 94, Pistons 83	Jordan (22)	Grant (10)
5/21	BULLS 105, Pistons 97	Jordan (35)	Pippen (10)
5/25	Bulls 113, PISTONS 107	Jordan (33)	Pippen (10)
5/27	Bulls 115, PISTONS 94	Jordan (29)	Grant (9)

NBA Finals: Bulls beat Lakers 4-1

Date	Score	Top Bulls scorer	Top rebounder
6/2	Lakers 93, BULLS 91	Jordan (36)	Grant (10)
6/5	BULLS 107, Lakers 86	Jordan (33)	Jordan, Perdue (7)
6/7	Bulls 104, LAKERS 96,OT	Jordan (29)	Pippen (13)
6/9	Bulls 97, LAKERS 82	Jordan (28)	Pippen (9)
6/12	Bulls 108, LAKERS 101	Pippen (32)	Pippen (13)

EAM

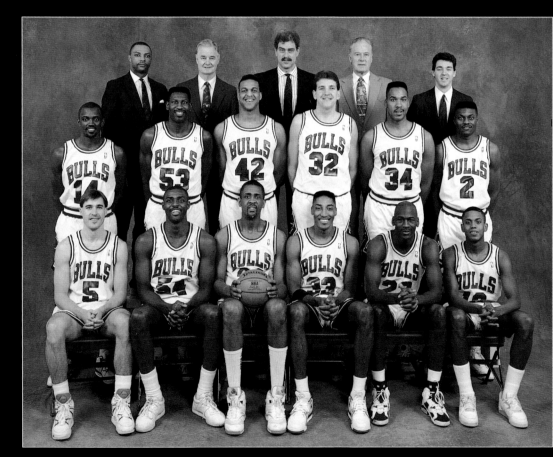

Back row (left to right): Jim Cleamons, Tex Winter, Phil Jackson, John Bach, Chip Schaefer. Middle row: Craig Hodges, Cliff Levingston, Scott Williams, Will Perdue, Stacey King, Dennis Hopson. Front row: John Paxson, Horace Grant, Bill Cartwright, Scottie Pippen, Michael Jordan, B.J. Armstrong.
PHOTO BY BILL SMITH

Jordan's 1990-91 A Ringing Success

All in all, it was not a bad year for Michael Jordan. He welcomed his second son into the world, had a hamburger named after him, won his fifth straight scoring title, agreed to let a network use his likeness in a Saturday morning cartoon,

earned his second Most Valuable Player award, cut a commercial with Little Richard, scored 21 points in one quarter, grabbed 19 rebounds in one game and hit a free throw with his eyes closed.

Oh, and one other thing.

He finally got the ring. The championship ring.

"I'm going to pass it on down to my kids," said an exuberant Jordan afterward. "No one can take it away from me. I don't know if I'll ever have this feeling again. All the things I've gone through, all the things the city has gone through. It was a lot of hard work, and what you see is the emotions of all that hard work paying off."

The Bulls' championship season gave Jordan a hat trick of sorts. He helped North Carolina beat George-town for the NCAA title in 1982, hitting the game-winning jumper to cap his freshman season. In the 1984 Olympics, he started on the U.S. team that won the gold medal, but waited seven years to experience that championship season again.

"Michael Jordan has proven on every level that he can win," said John Paxson. "Three or four years ago, we depended on Michael to pull us out down the stretch. That was unfair to him."

In the intense back-and-forth Game 5 with the Lakers, all eyes in the Forum were on Jordan to take the game under his control, just as he has done unflinchingly throughout his career with last-second baskets for the Bulls.

This time, however, it was Jordan the defender who

By Paul Sullivan

made two key steals in a 52-second span and the score tied with under six minutes left. And it was Jordan the rebounder who leaped high to grab a Tony Smith miss that led to Paxson's go-ahead 19-footer with 3:54 left. And it was Jordan the playmaker who fed Paxson for two game-sealing jumpers in the final 3:30.

Jordan thanked his teammates, the supporting cast who came out of his shadow and opened the eyes of a national television audience. He thanked his coach, whose patience and understanding were immeasurably important ingredients toward the maturation of the young Bulls' players.

"Phil has been a very unique coach," he said. "He reminds me of Coach [Dean] Smith. They both use psychology to bring out the best in you. This time, it paid off."

Now that the stigma has been removed, and Jordan has played for an NBA championship team despite the cries of the media that a league-leading scorer cannot pull a team to the top spot, Jordan will have another burden to carry.

At least that's the prognosis of his proud father, James, who warned everyone after the locker room celebration that a new and improved Michael Jordan is on the horizon.

"Now that he's got over the burden of winning a championship," said James Jordan, "he can play a lot more relaxed now. Totally relaxed. And that's a very scary situation." ∎

23

How do you spell Jordan? How about MVP? He was named the NBA's Most Valuable Player in 1990-91 for the second time and led the league in scoring for the fifth straight year, averaging 31.5 points a game.

He is the Bulls' all-time points leader with 16,596 and the only player besides Wilt Chamberlain to score more than 3,000 points in a season (3,041 in 1986-87). He reached the 15,000-point mark faster than any player in history other than Chamberlain. Jordan was named NBA Rookie of the Year in 1984-85.

33

This fourth-year player from Central Arkansas averaged 21.6 points and 8.9 rebounds a game in the 1991 playoffs. He topped the Bulls with 32 points in Game 5 of the NBA Finals.

Pippen, who came to the Bulls in June 1987 in a trade of drafting rights with Seattle, achieved his first triple-double in 1990 against Milwaukee with 17 points, 13 assists and 10 rebounds. He averaged 17.8 points a game during the regular season.

54

Clemson produced this 1987 first-round draft choice who has led the Bulls in rebounding for three straight seasons. He averaged 8.5 rebounds a game for the 1990-91 season, along with a scoring average of 12.8 points a game.

His single-game scoring high was 25 points. Grant made 58 percent of his shots during the playoffs, when he averaged 13.3 points a game.

24

Like Bill Russell, a center of legendary performance, Bill Cartwright came out of the University of San Francisco. The Bulls traded Charles Oakley and switched picks with New York in the 1988 draft to pry Cartwright away from the Knicks.

Cartwright averaged 9.5 points a game in the '91 playoffs. He scored his 10,000th NBA point Nov. 4, 1989, against the Boston Celtics.

5

For a player signed as a free agent (in October 1985), John Paxson has proven to be a steady performer. Sometimes he can be spectacular.

In the closing minutes of Game 5 against the Lakers in the NBA Finals, he scored 10 of the Bulls' 12 points.

Paxson, out of Notre Dame, averaged 8.7 points a game in the 1990-91 season, but he scored in double figures 42 times. He finished 10th in the league in field-goal percentage (54.8).

10

53

One of the key Bulls off the bench, B.J. Armstrong raised his scoring average by three points in 1990-91, the biggest improvement on the team.

Armstrong, a first-round draft pick out of Iowa, saw action in all 19 playoff games.

He had his biggest night as a pro on Dec. 23, when he scored 20 points.

Cliff Levingston hit his stride in the playoffs, contributing 45 points, 41 rebounds and seven assists. In Game 3 of the NBA Finals, he took over for the foul-plagued Scottie Pippen and hit five of five shots, grabbed four rebounds and recorded three blocks. He was signed before the season as a free agent.

WILL PERDUE

32

Will Perdue improved in every major statistical category while earning the position as a valued player off the bench. He set personal bests of 16 points in a regular-season game and 15 points in a playoff game. Perdue played in 74 games in 1990-91.

CRAIG HODGES

14

A high point of Craig Hodges' season was winning the three-point shooting contest before the NBA All-Star game. But Hodges is well-known for his long-range gunning. He contributed 11 three-pointers during the playoffs and is the Bulls' all-time three-point shot leader.

34 | 2

Stacey King endured a long season in 1990-91 after showing promise in his rookie year. In 1989-90, King was a second-team all-rookie pick. In the 1990 second-round playoffs against the 76ers, he scored 21 points. King, out of Oklahoma, was the Bulls' top draft pick in 1989.

Adjusting to a new team proved difficult for Dennis Hopson, the Nets' first-round draft pick in 1987 out of Ohio State. Injuries slowed the former Big 10 player of the year; he saw action in just 61 regular-season games and five playoff games.

42

COACH

The new kid on the block, Scott Williams, enjoyed an NBA title in his first season. Signed as a free agent out of North Carolina, he saw action in 51 games. Off the bench, Williams hit six of 13 shots and grabbed 20 rebounds in 12 playoff games.

League championships were nothing new to Phil Jackson. This two-time All-American out of North Dakota played on the Knicks' championship squad in 1973. Jackson honed his coaching skills in five seasons as a CBA coach, then served as an NBA assistant for five more years before getting the Bulls' job in July 1989.

A VALUABLE ASSIST

Phil Jackson was asked to assess the value of his assistant coaches. He laughed and said, "I can go on for 15 minutes," which he nearly did.

But in one sentence, he summed up the life of an assistant.

"They're underpaid and undernoticed guys," Jackson said, "and they're great to have around."

While Jackson has been in the spotlight, this championship also belongs to his assistant coaches, John Bach, Tex Winter and Jim Cleamons. They are the coaches working in the background, devising game plans, editing videotape, scouting, motivating and soothing wounded egos. Whatever needs to be done, they do it.

Yet for all the Bulls' success this year, none of those coaches will walk into a restaurant and create a stir. Only the most avid of Bulls fans know who they are.

But to hear General Manager Jerry Krause talk, Bach, Winter and Cleamons are as valuable as Jordan, Pippen and Grant.

"We've got the best coaching staff in basketball," said Krause of his pride and joy. "They bring to us so much experience and brilliance."

Few staffs can match the Bulls' for experience. Winter just completed his 44th season of coaching, while Bach finished his 40th.

Cleamons rounds out the staff as the relative rookie, finishing his second year with the team. His resume includes being a head coach at Youngstown State.

The coach's roles are well-defined. Bach is the defensive specialist, while Winter sets up the offense. Cleamons concentrates on scouting, along with keeping an eye on the younger players.

The trio are wonderfully diverse, according to Krause: "John is militaristic and hard-nosed. And Tex delves into theory, a sort of absent-minded professor. Jim is the hard-working bulldog, who picks the brains of the older guys."

Bach says the merger has formed a unique chemistry. He maintains it has been Jackson who has pulled it all together. Unlike other head coaches who might operate in a vacuum, Jackson relies heavily on his assistants and gives them a wide range of latitude.

"Some coaches are dogmatic, but not Phil," Bach said.

A case in point was Game 2 of the Finals. After watching film of Game 1, which the Bulls lost by two points, Bach reviewed the tape and came up with an idea. "I said, 'Let's go in this area with a double team,'" said Bach, who wouldn't reveal the specifics. "We did it and it worked. Phil listens. He makes everyone feel a part of the team."

This title has been particularly gratifying for Winter. He planned to retire after working for Dale Brown at LSU, but Krause convinced him to join the Bulls' staff in 1985.

Now, after 44 years in the business, Winter has reached the high-point in his career.

"At this stage, this could be my last opportunity to be involved," Winter said.

The same holds true for Bach, who also has seen more than his share of gyms. He's got his championship ring. It doesn't matter to him whether it came as an assistant or head coach. "People ask if I miss being a head coach. I don't. I don't crave the spotlight. Being in this situation could be the culmination of anyone's hopes. Believe me, this is big enough to go around." –ED SHERMAN

Bulls scout Jim Stack hugs Michael Jordan in the locker room after the Game 5 win. General Manager Jerry Krause (left) hugs the championship trophy.
PHOTOS BY CHARLES CHERNEY AND JOHN KRINGAS (LEFT)

'They're underpaid and undernoticed . . . and great to have around.'
-Bulls coach Phil Jackson, when asked the value of his assistants.

Bulls 1990-91 regular-season statistics

Player	Gm.	Avg. min.	FG-att	Pct	3 pt-att	FT-att	Pct.	Pts	Avg pts	Hi gm
Michael Jordan	82	37.0	990-1837	.539	29-93	571-671	.851	2580	31.5	46
Scottie Pippen	82	36.8	600-1153	.520	21-68	240-340	.706	1461	17.8	43
Horace Grant	78	33.9	401-733	.547	1-6	197-277	.711	1000	12.8	25
Bill Cartwright	79	28.8	318-649	.490	0-0	124-178	.697	760	9.6	20
B.J. Armstrong	82	21.1	304-632	.481	15-30	97-111	.874	720	8.8	19
John Paxson	82	24.0	317-578	.548	42-96	34-41	.829	710	8.7	28
Stacey King	76	15.8	156-334	.467	0-2	107-52	.704	419	5.5	16
Craig Hodges	73	11.5	146-344	.424	44-115	26-27	.963	362	5.0	20
Dennis Hopson	61	11.9	104-244	.426	1-5	55-83	.663	264	4.3	14
Will Perdue	74	13.1	115-235	.494	0-3	75-112	.670	307	4.1	15
Cliff Levingston	78	13.0	127-282	.450	1-4	59-91	.648	314	4.0	14
Scott Williams	51	6.6	53-104	.510	1-2	20-28	.714	127	2.5	10
BULLS	82	240.9	3632-7125	.510	155-424	1605-2111	.760	9024	110.0	155
Opponents	82	240.9	3267-6884	.475	190-626	1554-2017	.770	8278	101.0	145

Player	Off reb	Def reb	Tot reb	Reb avg	Ast	Ast avg	PF	DQ	Stls	Turnovers	Blkd shots
Michael Jordan	118	374	492	6.0	453	5.5	229	1	223	202	83
Scottie Pippen	163	432	595	7.3	511	6.2	270	3	193	232	93
Horace Grant	266	393	659	8.4	178	2.3	203	2	95	92	69
Bill Cartwright	167	319	486	6.2	126	1.6	167	0	32	113	15
B.J. Armstrong	25	124	149	1.8	301	3.7	118	0	70	107	4
John Paxson	15	76	91	1.1	297	3.6	136	0	62	69	3
Stacey King	72	136	208	2.7	65	0.9	134	0	24	91	42
Craig Hodges	10	32	42	0.6	97	1.3	74	0	34	35	2
Dennis Hopson	49	60	109	1.8	65	1.1	79	0	25	59	14
Will Perdue	122	214	336	4.5	47	0.6	147	1	23	75	57
Cliff Levingston	99	126	225	2.9	56	0.7	143	0	29	50	43
Scott Williams	42	56	98	1.9	16	0.3	51	0	12	23	13
BULLS	1148	2342	3490	42.6	2212	27.0	1751	7	822	1184	438
Opponents	1062	2162	3224	39.3	2016	24.6	1826	17	633	1402	348

Bulls 1991 playoff statistics

Player	Gm	Avg min	FG-att	Pct	3 pt-att	FT-att	Pct	Pts	Avg pts	Hi gm
Michael Jordan	17	40.5	197-376	.524	10-26	125-148	.845	529	31.1	46
Scottie Pippen	17	41.4	142-282	.504	4-17	80-101	.792	368	21.6	32
Horace Grant	17	39.2	91-156	.583	0-0	44-60	.733	226	13.3	22
Bill Cartwright	17	30.1	70-135	.519	0-0	22-32	.688	162	9.5	16
John Paxson	17	28.6	62-117	.530	2-14	14-14	1.000	140	8.2	20
B.J. Armstrong	17	16.1	35-70	.500	3-5	20-25	.800	93	5.5	18
Craig Hodges	17	12.3	33-78	.423	11-28	3-4	.750	80	4.7	16
Will Perdue	17	11.6	29-53	.547	0-0	12-22	.545	70	4.1	16
Cliff Levingston	17	11.3	21-41	.512	0-0	3-6	.500	45	2.6	10
Stacey King	11	7.8	8-27	.296	0-1	7-11	.636	23	2.1	4
Scott Williams	12	6.0	6-13	.462	0-1	11-20	.550	23	1.9	5
Dennis Hopson	5	3.6	2-6	.333	0-0	4-9	.444	8	1.6	3
BULLS	17	241.5	696-1354	.514	30-92	245-452	.763	1767	103.9	126
Opponents	17	241.5	574-1275	.450	50-152	370-461	.803	1568	92.2	107

Player	Off reb	Def reb	Tot reb	Reb avg	Ast	Ast avg	PF	DQ	Stls	Turnovers	Blkd shots
Michael Jordan	18	90	108	6.4	142	8.4	53	0	40	43	23
Scottie Pippen	37	114	151	8.9	99	5.8	58	1	42	55	19
Horace Grant	56	82	138	8.1	38	2.2	45	0	15	20	6
Bill Cartwright	25	55	80	4.7	32	1.9	55	0	9	21	7
John Paxson	2	21	23	1.4	53	3.1	32	0	11	6	0
B.J. Armstrong	5	22	27	1.6	43	2.5	13	0	19	13	1
Craig Hodges	0	4	4	0.2	10	0.6	21	0	11	11	0
Will Perdue	32	33	65	3.8	4	0.2	41	1	2	14	8
Cliff Levingston	22	19	41	2.4	7	0.4	28	0	10	2	7
Stacey King	9	13	22	2.0	2	0.2	15	0	1	9	1
Scott Williams	4	16	20	1.7	3	0.3	15	0	1	4	3
Dennis Hopson	2	2	4	0.8	1	0.2	2	0	1	1	1
BULLS	212	471	683	40.2	434	25.5	378	2	161	212	76
Opponents	198	413	611	35.9	327	19.2	396	5	115	270	65

1990-91 Final NBA standings

Eastern Conference
Central

Division	W	L	Pct	Home	Away
CHICAGO	61	21	.744	35-6	26-15
Detroit	50	32	.610	32-9	18-23
Milwaukee	48	34	.585	33-8	15-26
Atlanta	43	39	.524	29-12	14-27
Indiana	41	41	.500	29-12	12-29
Cleveland	33	49	.402	23-18	10-31
Charlotte	26	56	.317	17-24	9-32

Atlantic
Division

	W	L	Pct	Home	Away
Boston	56	26	.683	35-6	21-20
Philadelphia	44	38	.537	29-12	15-26
New York	39	43	.476	21-20	18-23
Washington	30	52	.366	21-20	9-32
New Jersey	26	56	.317	20-21	6-35
Miami	24	58	.293	18-23	6-35

Western Conference
Midwest

Division	W	L	Pct	Home	Away
San Antonio	55	27	.671	33-8	22-19
Utah	54	28	.659	36-5	18-23
Houston	52	30	.634	31-10	21-20
Orlando	31	51	.378	24-17	7-34
Minnesota	29	53	.354	21-20	8-33
Dallas	28	54	.341	20-21	8-33
Denver	20	62	.244	17-24	3-37

Pacific
Division

	W	L	Pct	Home	Away
Portland	63	19	.768	36-5	27-14
L.A. Lakers	57	24	.704	32-8	25-16
Phoenix	55	27	.671	32-9	23-18
Golden State	44	38	.537	30-11	14-27
Seattle	41	40	.506	28-13	13-27
L.A. Clippers	31	51	.378	23-18	8-33
Sacramento	25	57	.305	24-17	1-40

Bulls playoff history

Bulls did not reach the playoffs in 1968-69; 1975-76; 1977-78; 1978-79; 1979-80; 1981-82; 1982-83; 1983-84

1966-67—Eliminated by St. Louis 3-0 in first round.
1967-68—Eliminated by Los Angeles 4-1 in first round.
1969-70—Eliminated by Atlanta 4-1 in first round.
1970-71—Eliminated by Los Angeles 4-3 in first round.
1971-72—Eliminated by Los Angeles 4-0 in first round.
1972-73—Eliminated by Los Angeles 4-3 in first round.
1973-74—Beat Detroit 4-3 in first round. Eliminated by Milwaukee 4-0 in Western Conference finals.
1974-75—Beat Kansas City-Omaha 4-2 in first round. Eliminated by Golden State 4-3 in Western Conference finals.
1976-77—Eliminated by Portland 2-1 in first round.
1980-81—Beat New York 2-0 in first round. Eliminated by Boston 4-0 in Eastern Conference semifinals.

1991 NBA playoff glance

Eastern Conference
First round (best-of-5)
Bulls defeat New York 3-0

BULLS 126, New York 85	
BULLS 89, New York 79	
Bulls103, NEW YORK 94	

Boston defeats Indiana 3-2

BOSTON 127, Indiana 120
Indiana 130, BOSTON 118
Boston 112, INDIANA 105
INDIANA 116, Boston 113
BOSTON 124, Indiana 121

Detroit defeats Atlanta 3-2

Atlanta 103, DETROIT 98
DETROIT 101, Atlanta 88
Detroit 103, ATLANTA 91
ATLANTA 123, Detroit 111
DETROIT 113, Atlanta 81

Philadelphia defeats Milwaukee 3-0

Philadelphia 99, MILWAUKEE 90
Philadelphia 116, MILWAUKEE 112,OT
PHILADELPHIA 121, Milwaukee 100

Western Conference
First round (best-of-5)
Portland defeats Seattle 3-2

PORTLAND 110, Seattle 102
PORTLAND 115, Seattle 106
SEATTLE 102, Portland 99
SEATTLE 101, Portland 89
PORTLAND 119, Seattle 107

Golden State defeats San Antonio 3-1

SAN ANTONIO 130, Golden State 121
Golden State 111, SAN ANTONIO 98
GOLDEN STATE 109, San Antonio 106
GOLDEN STATE 110, San Antonio 97

LA Lakers defeat Houston 3-0

LA LAKERS 94, Houston 92
LA LAKERS 109, Houston 98
LA Lakers 94, HOUSTON 90

Utah defeats Phoenix 3-1

Utah 129, Phoenix 90
Phoenix 102, Utah 92
UTAH107, Phoenix 98
UTAH101, Phoenix 93

Eastern Conference
Semifinals (best-of-7)
Bulls defeat Philadelphia 4-1

BULLS 105, Philadelphia 92
BULLS 112, Philadelphia 100
PHILADELPHIA 99, Bulls 97
Bulls 101, PHILADELPHIA 85
BULLS 100, Philadelphia 95

Home team all caps

Detroit defeats Boston 4-2

Detroit 86, BOSTON 75
BOSTON 109, Detroit 103
Boston 115, DETROIT 83
DETROIT 104, Boston 97
Detroit 116, BOSTON 111
DETROIT 117, Boston 113, OT

Western Conference
Semifinals (best-of-7)
LA Lakers defeat Golden State 4-1

LA LAKERS 126, Golden State 116
Golden State 125, LA LAKERS 124
LA Lakers 115, GOLDEN STATE 112
LA Lakers 123, GOLDEN STATE 107
LA LAKERS 124,Golden State 119, OT

Portland defeats Utah 4-1

PORTLAND 117, Utah 97
PORTLAND 118, Utah 116
UTAH 107, Portland 101
Portland 104, UTAH 101
PORTLAND 103, Utah 96

Eastern Conference
Finals (best-of-7)
Bulls defeat Detroit 4-0

BULLS 94, Detroit 83
BULLS 105, Detroit 97
Bulls 113, DETROIT 107
Bulls 115, DETROIT 94

Western Conference
Finals (best-of-7)
LA Lakers defeat Portland 4-2

LA Lakers 111, PORTLAND 106
PORTLAND 109, LA Lakers 98
LA LAKERS 106, Portland 92
LA LAKERS 116, Portland 95
PORTLAND 95, LA Lakers 84
LA LAKERS 91, Portland 90

NBA Finals (best-of-7)
Bulls defeat LA Lakers 4-1

Sunday, June 2
LA Lakers 93, BULLS 91
Wednesday, June 5
BULLS 107, LA Lakers 86
Friday, June 7
Bulls 104, LA LAKERS 96
Sunday, June 9
Bulls 97, LA LAKERS 82
Wednesday, June 12
Bulls 108, LA LAKERS 101

1984-85—Eliminated by Milwaukee 3-1 in first round.
1985-86—Eliminated by Boston 3-0 in first round.
1986-87—Eliminated by Boston 3-0 in first round.
1987-88—Beat Cleveland 3-2 in first round. Eliminated by Detroit 4-1 in Eastern Conference semifinals.
1988-89—Beat Cleveland 3-2 in first round. Beat New York 4-2 in Eastern Conference semifinals. Eliminated by Detroit 4-2 in Eastern Conference finals.
1989-90—Beat Milwaukee 3-1 in first round. Beat Philadelphia 4-1 in Eastern Conference semifinals. Eliminated by Detroit 4-3 in Eastern Conference finals.
1990-91—Beat New York 3-0 in first round. Beat Philadelphia 4-1 in Eastern Conference semifinals. Beat Detroit 4-0 in Eastern Conference finals. Beat Los Angeles 4-1 in NBA Finals.

STAMPEDE! Staff

EDITOR: Bob Condor
CREATIVE DIRECTOR: Tony Majeri
ART DIRECTOR: Therese Shechter
PICTURE EDITOR: Tim Broekema
DESIGNER: Steven Bialer
ASSISTANT EDITORS: K.C. Johnson, Michael O'Donnell
SYSTEMS EDITOR: Ken Waller

The following people contributed to the Chicago Tribune's coverage of the 1990-91 championship season of the Chicago Bulls:

SPORTS
Associate Managing Editor/Sports: Richard Leslie
Sports Editor: Bob Condor
Associate Editors: Bill Hageman, Jim Masek, Ken Paxson
Assistant Editors: Jim Binkley, Tom Carkeek, Joseph Knowles
Reporters: Sam Smith, Paul Sullivan, Skip Myslenski, Mike Conklin, Melissa Isaacson, Robert Markus, Neil Milbert, Fred Mitchell, Steve Nidetz, Bob Sakamoto, Ed Sherman, Jorge Casuso
Columnists: Bernie Lincicome, Bob Verdi, Jerome Holtzman
Copy Editors: Bob Fischer, Dan Gibbard, Julie Hanna, Jim Harding, K.C. Johnson, Michael Kates, Chris Kuc, Rich La Susa, Rebecca Morrissey, Dan Moulton, Gary Reinmuth, Mark Shapiro, Ed Stone, Rich Strom, Jack Thompson, Tim Tierney, Bob Vanderberg
Makeup: Rick Maupin, Gene McCormick, Mike Hanlon, Mike Esposito, Norm Unger, John Blais
Editorial Assistants: Claudia Banks, Cynthia Curry-Bennett, Tony Tranchita
Staff: Bernie Colbeck, Rose Halligan, Steve Mauzer

PHOTOGRAPHY
Director of Photography: Phil Greer
Chief Photographer: Jose More
Picture Editor: Karen Engstrom
Assignment Editor: Don Bierman
Assistant Picture Editors: Tim Broekema, Milbert Brown, Mark Hinajosa, Wendy White
Photographers: Charles Cherney, Eduardo Contreras, Michael Fryer, John Kringas, Bob Langer, Michael Meinhardt, Charles Osgood, Jim Prisching, Nancy Stone, George Thompson, Ed Wagner
Photo Lab Technicians: Jim Badali, Olavs Borg, Kathleen Celer, Prisana Kongsuwan, Anthony Simmons, Art Walker

GRAPHICS
Associate Managing Editor/Photo, Art, Graphics: George Langford
Creative Director: Tony Majeri
Illustrations Editor: Stephen Cvengros
Artists: Paige Braddock, Vasin Omer D., Scott Holingue, Tom Irvine, Annette Ney Meade, Dennis Odom, Stephen Ravenscraft, Nancy I. Z. Reese, Enrique Rodriguez, Don Sena, Julie Sheer, Rick Tuma, Terry Volpp

RESEARCH
Photos: Mary Wilson, Judi Marriott, Amanda Vogt, Dianna Sonoras, Abby DeShane, Jonas Baltrukonis, Donna Johnson, Steve Marino, Cynthia Marshall
Editorial Material: Karen Blair, Alan Peters, Mary Huschen, Joe Pete, Barbara Sherlock

PRE-PRESS
Color Prepress Department Manager: Bruce Wade
Color Prepress Supervisor: James P. Conner
Planners: Lisa Dortch, Andre Clark
Proofer/Plotters: Jose Trevino, Eric Shiplock, Ron Garde, Jennifer Baas
Color Systems Operators: Mike Luczak, Tom Gruzlewski, Terri Sticha, William Glenn
Color Scanner Operators: Laura Delaurentis, Joseph Lamantia, James Jurewicz, Karen Merwick

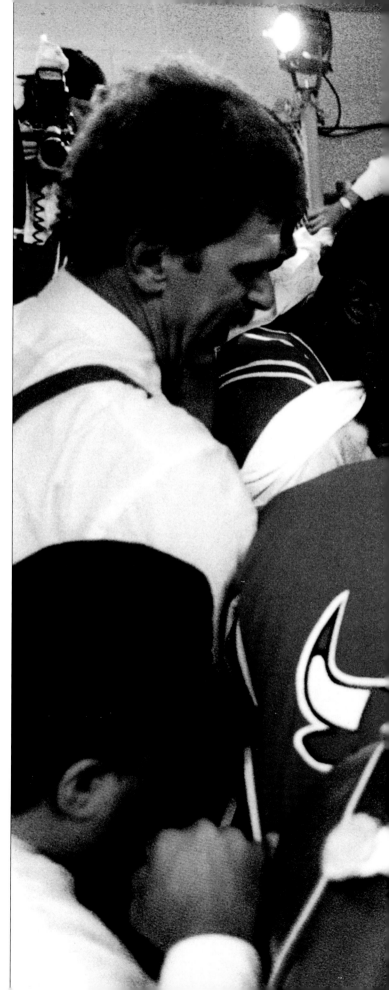

After the series-clinching win over the Lakers, the Bulls conduct a team prayer.
PHOTO BY CHARLES CHERNEY

PHOTO BY CHARLES CHERNEY

It means
so much. Not just for me
but for this city.